ONE STOP

The One Stop Series

Series editor: David Martin, FCIS, FIPD, FCB
Buddenbrook Consultancy

A series of practical, user-friendly yet authoritative titles designed to provide a one stop guide to key topics in business administration.

Other books in the series to date include:

David Martin	*One Stop Company Secretary*
David Martin	*One Stop Personnel*
Jeremy Stranks	*One Stop Health and Safety*
John Wyborn	*One Stop Contracts*
David Martin	*One Stop Property*
Harris Rosenberg	*One Stop Finance*
Robert Leach	*One Stop Payroll*
David Martin/ John Wyborn	*One Stop Negotiation*

1998 Titles

David Martin	*One Stop Communication*
Robin Ellison	*One Stop Pensions*
Patrick Forsyth	*One Stop Marketing*
David Martin	*One Stop Customer Care*

ONE STOP
Insurance

KAREN HUNTINGFORD

ICSA Publishing
The Official Publishing Company of
The Institute of Chartered Secretaries and Administrators

in association with

Prentice Hall Europe

London New York Toronto Sydney Tokyo Singapore
Madrid Mexico City Munich Paris

First published 1998 by
ICSA Publishing Limited
Campus 400, Maylands Avenue
Hemel Hempstead
Hertfordshire, HP2 7EZ

Typeset in 10/12.5 pt Meridien with Frutiger Light
by Hart McLeod, Cambridge

Printed and bound in Great Britain
by MPG Books Ltd, Bodmin, Cornwall

British Library Cataloguing in Publication Data

A catalogue record for this book is available from
the British Library

ISBN: 1-860-72044-7

1 2 3 4 5   02 01 00 99 98

Contents

Association of British Insurers

Introduction

The Association of British Insurers (ABI) represents the interests of its members to government, regulatory and other agencies. It provides a wide range of services for its members, who are made up of some 430 insurance companies and who between them account for over 90% of the business of UK insurance companies.

Objectives

Formed in 1985 following an amalgamation of smaller, specialist associations, the ABI's objectives are:

- to protect and promote the interests of members in respect of all classes of insurance business and in their related activities;
- to take concerted measures whenever the interests of members may be affected by the action of any government body or agency;
- to cooperate with any association having similar objectives.

Activities

The activities of the ABI include work on:

- the collection of relevant market statistics, e.g. policies in force, premium income, losses incurred;
- fire prevention;
- liability;
- fraud;
- motor accidents;
- vehicle groups;
- life underwriting;
- framing codes of conduct.

The General Insurance Council and the Life Assurance Council divide responsibility for this work between them. The ABI also has a public relations role, trying to increase public awareness and understanding of the different facets of insurance. In addition, it has produced codes of practice which lay down guidelines for the conduct of business between insurers, intermediaries and new or existing policyholders. These apply to personal contracts only, not to any commercial contracts.

Statements of Insurance Practice

There are two main codes of practice for insurance company operations – the Statement of General Insurance Practice and the Statement of Long-term Insurance Practice. They apply to policies taken out by people in a purely private capacity.

Both statements set out guidelines that member companies are expected to follow.

Checklist: Behavioural guidelines for ABI members

These guidelines relate to:

- the types of question that may be asked on PROPOSAL FORMS and the information to be given to prospective policyholders;
- the need for the declaration on a proposal form to refer to the fact that the policy has been completed to the best of the proposer's knowledge and belief, rather than that its contents are true;
- the need for a copy of the proposal form to be given to the policyholder before any query over its completion may be raised;
- timescales for notification of potential CLAIMS to insurers;
- repudiation of claims;
- prompt settlement of claims;
- the need for renewal instructions to make it clear that the duty of disclosure revives at renewal;
- the requirement that changes be made to insurance documents on reprinting to bring them into line with the Statement;
- disputes.

A copy of the Statement of General Insurance Practice is reproduced below. Its provisions mirror those in the Statement of Long-term Practice, which also includes industrial assurance policies.

ASSOCIATION OF BRITISH INSURERS

STATEMENT OF GENERAL INSURANCE PRACTICE

The following Statement of normal insurance practice applies to general insurances of policyholders resident in the UK and insured in their private capacity only.

1. **PROPOSAL FORMS**

    (a) The declaration at the foot of the proposal form should be restricted to completion according to the proposer's knowledge and belief.

    (b) Neither the proposal form nor the policy shall contain any provision converting the statements as to past or present fact in the proposal form into warranties. But insurers may require specific warranties about matters which are material to the risk.

    (c) If not included in the declaration, prominently displayed on the proposal form should be a statement:-

    　　(i)　drawing the attention of the proposer to the consequences of the failure to disclose all material facts, explained as those facts an insurer would regard as likely to influence the acceptance and assessment of the proposal;

    　　(ii)　warning that if the proposer is in any doubt about facts considered material, he should disclose them.

    (d) Those matters which insurers have found generally to be material will be the subject of clear questions in proposal forms.

    (e) So far as is practicable, insurers will avoid asking questions which would require expert knowledge beyond that which the proposer could reasonably be expected to possess or obtain or which would require a value judgement on the part of the proposer.

    (f) Unless the prospectus or the proposal form contains full details of the standard cover offered, and whether or not it contains an outline of that cover, the proposal form shall include a prominent statement that a specimen copy of the policy form is available on request.

    (g) Proposal forms shall contain a prominent warning that the proposer should keep a record (including copies of letters) of all information supplied to the insurer for the purpose of entering into the contract.

    (h) The proposal form shall contain a prominent statement that a copy of the completed form:-

    　　(i)　is automatically provided for retention at the time of completion; or

    　　(ii)　will be supplied as part of the insurer's normal practice: or

    　　(iii)　will be supplied on request within a period of three months after its completion.

    (i) An insurer shall not raise an issue under the proposal form, unless the policyholder is provided with a copy of the completed form.

2. **CLAIMS**

    (a) Under the conditions regarding notification of a claim, the policyholder shall not be asked to do more than report a claim and subsequent developments as soon as reasonably possible except in the case of legal processes and claims which a third party requires the policyholder to notify within a fixed time where immediate advice may be required.

    (b) An insurer will not repudiate liability to indemnify a policyholder:-

    　　(i)　on grounds of non-disclosure of a material fact which a policyholder could not reasonably be expected to have disclosed;

    　　(ii)　on grounds of misrepresentation unless it is a deliberate or negligent misrepresentation of a material fact;

(iii) on grounds of a breach of warranty or condition where the circumstances of the loss are unconnected with the breach unless fraud is involved.

Paragraph 2 (b) above does not apply to Marine and Aviation policies.

(c) Liability under the policy having been established and the amount payable by the insurer agreed, payment will be made without avoidable delay.

3. **RENEWALS**

(a) Renewal notices shall contain a warning about the duty of disclosure including the necessity to advise changes affecting the policy which have occurred since the policy inception or last renewal date, whichever was the later.

(b) Renewal notices shall contain a warning that the proposer should keep a record (including copies of letters) of all information supplied to the insurer for the purpose of renewal of the contract.

4. **COMMENCEMENT**

Any changes to insurance documents will be made as and when they need to be reprinted, but the Statement will apply in the meantime.

5. **POLICY DOCUMENTS**

Insurers will continue to develop clearer and more explicit proposal forms and policy documents whilst bearing in mind the legal nature of insurance contracts.

6. **DISPUTES**

The provisions of the Statement shall be taken into account in arbitration and any other referral procedures which may apply in the event of disputes between policyholders and insurers relating to matters dealt with in the Statement.

7. **EC**

This Statement will need reconsideration when the Draft EC Directive on Insurance Contract Law is adopted and implemented in the United Kingdom.

ASSOCIATION OF BRITISH INSURERS
51 Gresham Street, London EC2V 7HQ. Tel: 071-600 3333
Printed January 1986
(Reprinted January 1992)

Codes of Practice for intermediaries other than registered insurance brokers

The codes of practice set down a framework of general principles within which ABI members should sell insurance. As intermediaries are not part of the ABI, it is up to member companies to enforce the codes and to do their very best to ensure that anyone selling their policies observes the appropriate code's provisions. Withdrawal of the agency would be an insurer's final sanction against an intermediary who failed to abide by the guidelines set out in the relevant code of practice. Brokers must abide by the requirements of the Insurance Brokers Registration Council, which is why they are not included within this code of practice

As with the Statements of Insurance Practice there is a code of practice for intermediaries selling general insurance and another for those selling long-term insurance (non-investment business).

Checklist: Behavioural guidelines for intermediaries

The requirements of both general and long-term business intermediaries are similar and relate to:

- making appointments with prospective policyholders;
- giving professional advice;
- conduct during contacts with prospective policyholders;
- explaining the contract, charges and commissions;
- not influencing the disclosure of underwriting information;
- keeping proper accounts and dealing with money collected;
- documentation;
- existing policyholders falling within the code's remit;
- notification of potential claims to insurers.

The general insurance code requires all non-broker intermediaries to take out and maintain professional indemnity insurance. The minimum level of cover and other requirements are set out in an annex to the main code of practice.

The General Insurance Business Code of Practice is reproduced below.

Note: Both of these documents are reproduced with kind permission of the ABI, 51 Gresham Street, London, EC2V 7HQ

Association of British Insurers

GENERAL INSURANCE BUSINESS - CODE OF PRACTICE FOR ALL INTERMEDIARIES (INCLUDING EMPLOYEES OF INSURANCE COMPANIES) OTHER THAN REGISTERED INSURANCE BROKERS (INTRODUCED JANUARY 1989)

This Code applies to general business as defined in the Insurance Companies Act 1982, but does not apply to reinsurance business. As a condition of membership of the Association of British Insurers (ABI), members undertake to enforce this Code and to use their best endeavours to ensure that all those involved in selling their policies observe its provisions.

It shall be an overriding obligation of an intermediary at all times to conduct business with utmost good faith and integrity.

In the case of complaints from policyholders (either direct or indirect, for example through a trading standards officer or Citizens Advice Bureau), the insurance company concerned shall require an intermediary to co-operate so that the facts can be established. An intermediary shall inform the policyholder complaining that he can take his problem direct to the insurance company concerned.

NOTE:- The Code provides a framework of general principles within which ABI members and intermediaries should sell general insurance products eg motor, household, creditor (payment protection), travel, private medical etc.

ABI has issued guidance to accompany the Code, which is issued periodically to its members. The interpretation of the requirements will vary according to the particular type of insurance and the circumstances of the customer.

A leaflet setting out the respective responsibilities of the intermediary and insurer can be obtained from your insurer, through your intermediary, or direct from ABI at 51 Gresham Street, London EC2V 7HQ.

ABI will also supply a resumé of the guidance issued to its members on request.

GENERAL SALES PRINCIPLES

1. The intermediary shall:-

    (i) where appropriate, make a prior appointment to call. Unsolicited or unarranged calls shall be made at an hour likely to be suitable to the prospective policyholder;

    (ii) when he makes contact with the prospective policyholder, identify himself and explain as soon as possible that the arrangements he wishes to discuss could include insurance. He shall make it known that he is:-

    (a) an employee of an insurance company, for whose conduct the company accepts responsibility; or

    (b) an agent of one company, for whose conduct the company accepts responsibility; or

    (c) an agent of two or up to six companies, for whose conduct the companies accept responsibility; or

    (d) an independent intermediary seeking to act on behalf of the prospective policyholder, for whose conduct the company/companies do not accept responsibility;

    (iii) ensure as far as possible that the policy proposed is suitable to the needs and resources of the prospective policyholder;

    (iv) give advice only on those insurance matters in which he is knowledgeable and seek or recommend other specialist advice when necessary; and

    (v) treat all information supplied by the prospective policyholder as completely confidential to himself and to the company or companies to which the business is being offered.

2. The intermediary shall not:-

    (i) inform the prospective policyholder that his name has been given by another person, unless he is prepared to disclose that person's name if requested to do so by the prospective policyholder and has that person's consent to make that disclosure;

    (ii) make inaccurate or unfair criticisms of any insurer; or

    (iii) make comparisons with other types of policy unless he makes clear the differing characteristics of each policy.

B   EXPLANATION OF THE CONTRACT

The intermediary shall:-

(i)   identify the insurance company;

(ii) explain all the essential provisions of the cover afforded by the policy, or policies, which he is recommending, so as to ensure as far as possible that the prospective policyholder understands what he is buying;

(iii) draw attention to any restrictions and exclusions applying to the policy;

(iv) if necessary, obtain from the insurance company specialist advice in relation to items (ii) and (iii) above;

(v)   not impose any charge in addition to the premium required by the insurance company without disclosing the amount and purpose of such charge; and

(vi) if he is an independent intermediary, disclose his commission on request.

C   DISCLOSURE OF UNDERWRITING INFORMATION

The intermediary shall, in obtaining the completion of the proposal form or any other material:-

(i)   avoid influencing the prospective policyholder and make it clear that all the answers or statements are the latter's own responsibility; and

(ii) ensure that the consequences of non-disclosure and inaccuracies are pointed out to the prospective policyholder by drawing his attention to the relevant statement in the proposal form and by explaining them himself to the prospective policyholder.

D   ACCOUNTS AND FINANCIAL ASPECTS

The intermediary shall, if authorised to collect monies in accordance with the terms of his agency appointment:-

(i)   keep a proper account of all financial transactions with a prospective policyholder which involve the transmission of money in respect of insurance;

(ii) acknowledge receipt (which, unless the intermediary has been otherwise authorised by the insurance company, shall be on his own behalf) of all money received in connection with an insurance policy and shall distinguish the premium from any other payment included in the money; and

(iii) remit any such monies so collected in strict conformity with his agency appointment.

E   DOCUMENTATION

The intermediary shall not withhold from the policyholder any written evidence or documentation relating to the contract of insurance.

F   EXISTING POLICYHOLDERS

The intermediary shall abide by the principles set out in this Code to the extent that they are relevant to his dealings with existing policyholders.

G   CLAIMS

If the policyholder advises the intermediary of an incident which might give rise to a claim, the intermediary shall inform the company without delay, and in any event within three working days, and thereafter give prompt advice to the policyholder of the company's requirements concerning the claim, including the provision as soon as possible of information required to establish the nature and extent of the loss. Information received from the policyholder shall be passed to the company without delay.

H   PROFESSIONAL INDEMNITY COVER FOR INDEPENDENT INTERMEDIARIES

The intermediary shall obtain, and maintain in force, professional indemnity insurance in accordance with the requirements of ABI as set out in the Annex, which may be updated from time to time.

I   LETTERS OF APPOINTMENT

This Code of Practice shall be incorporated verbatim or by reference in all Letters of Appointment of non-registered intermediaries and no policy of the company shall be sold by such intermediaries except within the terms of such a Letter of Appointment.

Average

Introduction

Average is an insurance practice that aims to ensure that those taking out insurance obtain cover for the full value at risk. It operates to reduce the amount of a claim payment if underinsurance is found to exist at the time of a loss.

The Pro-rata Condition of Average

All fire insurances and other material damage policies are subject to the pro rata condition of average. This is shown in policies as the Condition of Average (Underinsurance).

Some insurances are exempt from average:

- private residences and personal effects;
- buildings used solely for public worship, halls and Sunday Schools;
- agricultural produce (the Special Condition of Average (Under-insurance) applies here instead);
- insurances subject to the Two Conditions of Average (Underinsurance);
- some insurances on buildings in the course of erection;
- rent insurance;
- first loss insurances.

Wording

If an item in the policy is declared subject to average, then this wording applies:

> Whenever a sum insured is declared to be subject to Average, if such a sum shall at the commencement of any DAMAGE be less than the value of the property covered within such sum insured, then the amount payable by the insurer in respect of such DAMAGE shall be proportionately reduced.

Objective

Average was introduced to prevent insurers being put at a disadvantage by someone taking out insurance for less than the full value of the property at risk. In so doing, the person contributes less premium to the common pool than the risk represents, but in the absence of average, would receive full indemnity for any partial loss.

Average imposes on the insured the obligation to bear part of every loss if underinsurance exists at the time of a loss. The true value at risk is an important question which a loss adjuster would attempt to establish on an insurer's behalf in the event of a loss.

The insured is liable to bear part of the loss in proportion to the relationship that the value at risk bears to the sum insured.

The formula used to work out an insurer's liability if average applies is:

$$\frac{\text{sum insured at time of loss}}{\text{full value at time of loss}} \quad \text{x} \quad \text{cost of repairs}$$

Case study

A small business suffers a fire which causes £15,000 of damage. The business has insured its premises for £50,000. On investigation of the claim, the insurer discovers the true value of the premises to be £75,000. In view of the underinsurance, the pro rata condition of average contained in the policy would apply. The insurer's contribution would be calculated as below:

$$\frac{\text{sum insured at time of loss} = £50,000}{\text{full value at time of loss} = £75,000} \quad \text{x} \quad \text{cost of repairs} = £15,000$$

therefore the insurer's contribution is $\frac{50,000}{75,000} \times 15,000 = £10,000$.

Special Condition of Average (Underinsurance)

This applies to agricultural produce. If the sum insured is more than 75% of the value at risk at the time of a loss, average will not apply.

If it is less than 75% of the true value at risk, then average applies in the normal way.

Two Conditions of Average (Underinsurance)

This applies where cover for contents or stock has been arranged on a floating basis (see FIRE AND SPECIAL PERILS INSURANCE).

It is a combination of the standard condition of average, the 'more specific insurance' condition common to general insurance policies (which relieves the insurer of liability under the policy if another policy exists which more specifically covers the property than the policy in question) and the CONTRIBUTION condition.

If a more specific policy does exist, the insurer of the first policy will only be liable to pay any value in excess of the loss covered by the more specific policy.

Buildings insurance

Introduction

Cover for damage to the fabric of a private dwelling is provided by a building insurance policy. (See FIRE AND SPECIAL PERILS INSURANCE for material damage cover for commercial premises.)

The term 'buildings' refers to the main structure and to any outbuildings such as garages, sheds, greenhouses, swimming pools and tennis courts. Also included within this cover would be damage to fitted kitchens, fitted wardrobes, electrical fittings, sanitary fittings and double glazing. The usual way to determine whether something falls within the scope of building insurance is to think about whether you would leave it behind when selling the property.

Checklist: Cover provided

Cover is usually available in respect of damage to the range of buildings identified above, caused by:

- fire, lightning, explosion and earthquake;
- riot, civil commotion, strikes, labour or political disturbances, malicious damage or vandalism;
- storm or flood;
- falling trees or branches;
- escape of water;
- escape of oil;
- theft or attempted theft;
- impact;
- subsidence, ground heave or landslip;
- breakage or collapse of television or radio receiving aerials, aerial fittings or masts;
- accidental damage to drains, pipes, cables or underground pipes;
- accidental breakage of glass and sanitary fixtures;
- legal fees, architects' and surveyors' fees, cost of debris removal;
- loss of rent.

Accidental damage cover is not automatically included, but is available as an extension, attracting a higher premium.

Restrictions

There are some restrictions on the cover provided:

- If the building is unfurnished or unoccupied for more than 30 days, cover in respect of malicious damage, escape of water or oil, theft or attempted theft and accidental breakage of fixed glass or sanitary fittings would be excluded.
- Storm or flood cover specifically excludes damage caused by frost, subsidence, ground heave or landslip and damage to walls, gates, fences or hedges. It is also often subject to an EXCESS.
- Cover for falling trees and branches specifically excludes damage to walls, gates, fences or hedges.
- Impact cover is likely specifically to exclude damage caused by pets.
- Subsidence, ground heave or landslip cover excludes damage caused by normal shrinkage or settlement, by faulty workmanship or design or faulty materials, by coastal or riverbank erosion, during demolition, repair or structural alteration, from movement of solid floor slabs independently of the foundations and to structures other than the house unless the house is damaged at the same time by the same cause. An excess is always imposed for this cover.
- Legal, architects' or surveyors' fees do not include the cost of preparing the insured's claim.
- A limit of 10–15% of the buildings sum assured applies to loss of rent cover.
- Damage whilst the building is let, or from wear and tear, settlement and shrinkage, wet or dry rot, fungus, vermin or insects would also be excluded.

Business interruption insurance

Introduction

In the event of a loss from material damage of some sort, a business, if properly insured, will be able to recoup its losses for the damage to property. There would remain, however, losses from the incident which would not be covered by a material damage policy. It is for these losses that the business interruption policy (previously also known as consequential loss) provides cover.

Material damage proviso

Most business interruption policies contain what is known as the 'material damage proviso', which is a requirement that insurance in respect of material damage must be in place before the business interruption policy becomes operative. The perils covered in the business interruption policy must correspondingly be covered in the material damage policy. It is, however, becoming more common for policies to be issued without this requirement.

Policy cover

The policy will supply cash to:

* pay maintenance charges, rent, rates, insurance;
* remunerate staff retained after the loss;
* meet redundancy costs and other notice costs for employees who have to be dismissed;
* cover the increase in cost of working after the loss;
* restore lost profit.

However, some losses will remain uninsured:

- depreciation of undamaged stock after a loss;
- failure to recover pre-loss debts;
- fines or penalty payments under contracts breached as a result of the loss;
- third party claims;
- loss of goodwill.

Claims under a business interruption policy relate either to increased cost of working or to loss of gross profit (see definitions checklist below).

Fire, all risks and engineering are the most common forms of business interruption policy. It will help your understanding of this subject if you first read the FIRE AND SPECIAL PERILS INSURANCE and ENGINEERING INSURANCE sections of this guide.

Fire

As noted under FIRE AND SPECIAL PERILS INSURANCE, the Association of British Insurers has issued wordings for some classes of material damage insurance. It has also produced a wording for business interruption, the Fire and Special Perils Policy (Business Interruption).

The standard fire perils are covered by the business interruption policy, which also covers non-domestic boilers. The special perils also correlate to the standard fire policy, but a further six special perils (all related to engineering) are covered:

- explosion and collapse of steam pipes;
- explosion of vessels;
- explosion and collapse of vessels;
- collapse of boilers;
- overheating of tubes;
- overheating of boilers and economisers.

All risks

The ABI also produces a Standard 'All Risks' Policy (Business Interruption). It is essential that cover is identical under both policies, because of the material damage proviso, and therefore material damage and business interruption are often insured under a combined all risks policy.

The same cover and exclusions apply to the business interruption policy as apply to the 'all risks' material damage policy.

Optional extensions

The policy can be extended to cover business interruption losses resulting from damage by the insured perils at premises other than those insured, e.g. customers' or suppliers' premises. An additional premium is payable for this cover.

It can also be extended to cover:

- specified suppliers: premises of named suppliers of components, goods or materials;
- unspecified suppliers;
- specified customers: on the basis of a set maximum trading amount;
- transit risks;
- prevention of access: if nearby premises are damaged or a bomb threat occurs;
- public utilities: damage at any utility supply premises which interrupts the insured's supply;
- notifiable disease, vermin, defective sanitary arrangements, murder and suicide.

Engineering

As for the material damage risk, there is no standard form for this cover, but the perils that the policy covers can be divided into those relating to failure of public utility supply and those relating to sudden and unforeseen damage from any accidental cause not specifically excluded.

Engineering business interruption policies usually exclude:

- the perils covered by the ABI Standard Fire and Special Perils Policy;
- the general market exclusions;
- a scheme which rations supplies of a supply authority;
- a deliberate act of a supply authority.

Indemnity period

A business interruption policy will specify a maximum indemnity period, chosen by the person taking out the insurance in line with his or her opinion of how long the business may be affected by an incident which interrupts its activities.

> **Warning**
>
> Note that the basis for selecting this period is how long the effects of the incident would be felt by the business, not how long it would take for the business to become operational again. If working in altered circumstances, profits or turnover could be reduced for some time after a business is able to recommence trading.

The indemnity period begins when the incident happens and ends when the specified period expires.

Policy wording

For all types of cover, the insurer agrees to pay the insured, on the basis set out in the specification, for any consequential loss following material damage by an insured peril.

Consequential loss is defined as: 'loss resulting from interruption of or interference with the business carried on by the insured at the premises in consequence of the loss or destruction of or damage to property used by the insured at the premises for the purposes of the business.'

General exclusions

As with the material damage policy, these are:

* war, riot, civil commotion;
* ionising radiation or radioactive contamination or explosive nuclear assembly;
* terrorism in Northern Ireland;
* pollution or contamination.

Conditions

The general conditions are:

* the policy is voidable in the event of misrepresentation or non-disclosure by the insured;
* any changes in the risk must be advised to the insurer, particularly if the business is wound up, or if the insured's interest in it ceases (except by death) or if the risk is increased.

The claims conditions are:

- action to be taken by the insured in the event of a claim;
- consequences of fraud;
- contribution;
- subrogation;
- arbitration.

The policy specification

Together with the policy wording and the schedule, the specification forms part of the business interruption contract. Its function is to set out the formula for the calculation of any consequential loss under the policy.

Checklist: Definitions

Working expenses: direct production costs and raw materials, both of which vary in line with levels of production.

Standing charges: fixed charges or overheads which do not vary in line with production levels.

Net profit: surplus available after payments for working expenses and standing charges have been made.

Turnover: income (or revenue, or sales, or fees).

Gross profit: the difference between turnover and working expenses.

Rate of gross profit: usually a percentage of turnover.

Additional expenditure: the increase in the cost of working made necessary by the loss.

Specification: Gross profits wording (sum insured basis)

The formula to be used for **reduction in turnover** is:

Standard turnover, minus turnover during indemnity period, multiplied by rate of gross profit.

The formula to be used for **increased cost of working** is:

Additional expenditure incurred to avoid or diminish the reduction in turnover which would have happened but for the expenditure. The maximum payment would be limited by the limit of the rate of gross profit multiplied by the reduction in turnover avoided.

Savings

Any amount saved by the cessation of work following the loss event is deducted from any payment in respect of consequential loss.

Average

The pro rata condition of AVERAGE applies to any underinsurance if the sum insured is less than the sum produced by the rate of gross profit multiplied by the annual turnover.

Specification: Gross profits wording (declaration-linked basis)

This is now the preferred method of calculating consequential losses.

The specification wording is the same as for the sum insured basis, except that the application of average to the policy is deleted. Instead, a limit is set on the insurer's liability for gross profit of 133% of the estimated gross profit, and for other items a limit of 100% of the stated sum insured applies.

The insured must provide details of estimated gross profit for the nearest financial year to the period of insurance at inception and renewal. A declaration of actual figures is then made at the end of the period of insurance and the premium is adjusted accordingly.

The declaration linked basis also provides that the insurer's liability would not reduce after a loss, but would be automatically reinstated, an additional premium then becoming due from the insured.

Calculation of sum insured

The sum insured is the gross profit that the business expects to make during the period of insurance. The assessment of gross profit must be based on existing audited accounts, projected into the future, with an adjustment made for the impact of inflation.

Two bases are favoured for this calculation:

- addition basis: net (or trading) profit plus insured standing charges;
- difference basis: turnover minus uninsured working expenses (those that will decrease when turnover decreases).

For the declaration-linked policy, an estimate of gross profit must be provided which would be the insured's estimate of gross profit for the financial year most nearly concurrent with the period of insurance, proportionately increased where the maximum indemnity period is more than 12 months.

Other specifications

Cover can also be provided on the basis of:

- gross revenue (income);
- gross rentals (from tenants);
- net takings or trading profit;
- increase in cost of working only.

Checklist: Risk assessment

Insurers will want to assess the following aspects of the physical risk:

- situation of premises and work/processes involved;
- fire spread risk;
- time required for repair or reinstatement following a loss.

Ideally the material damage and business interruption surveys would be conducted together.

The interruption risk would involve assessing the following physical aspects of the risk, plus the moral hazard:

- name and occupation of the insured;
- address of premises;
- details of trade or manufacturing processes;
- raw materials;
- other materials, e.g. packaging;
- machinery and plant;
- alternative arrangements;
- utilities and power;
- employees;
- customers;
- stockpiling;
- computers;
- regulations applicable to the replacement of buildings.

With all of this information available, the underwriter can work out the ESTIMATED MAXIMUM LOSS: the maximum probable business interruption loss arising out of the maximum possible material damage loss to the key interruption risk at the most critical time.

Case study

Think about a business that produces luxury diaries. It relies upon a single, specialist supplier for calf-leather binders, into which it places printed sheets. The supplier is insured against fire and special perils.

Now compare the effects of three incidents at the supplier's premises on the profits of the main business:

Fire 1: occurs in February in an outbuilding, causes a small amount of damage;

Fire 2: occurs in February, supplier's premises completely destroyed, no supplies for three months;

Fire 3: occurs in September, premises completely destroyed, no supplies for three months.

Fire 1 would not inconvenience the main business at all. Fire 2 would cause some inconvenience and possibly increased costs if alternative suppliers have to be found and similarly competitive rates cannot be negotiated.

Fire 3 is a disaster. This happens immediately before the main business goes into assembly and delivery of its prestige diaries for the New Year market. It has no time to source binders of similar quality from elsewhere and thus loses out on profits from its main income-generating opportunity.

This is the idea behind the EML – the financial consequences of the worst possible thing happening to the worst possible extent at the worst possible time.

Rating

From this information, a premium can be worked out. Each insurer will use its own method of arriving at what it considers to be an appropriate rate for the risk.

Certificate of insurance

Introduction

A certificate of insurance is proof of the existence of a contract of insurance, and is issued in respect of insurances that are compulsory.

The statute which makes the insurance compulsory also requires the issue of a certificate of insurance as proof that cover is in force. It may also specify the information that must be included on the certificate.

Motor insurance certificates

The requirement for the issue of a MOTOR INSURANCE certificate is set out in the current (1988) Road Traffic Act. The form of the certificate is set out in the Motor Vehicles (Third Party Risks) Regulations 1972, which require motor insurance certificates to carry:

- the registration mark of the vehicle (in which case the certificate is referred to as 'closed') or a description of the vehicle (known as a 'blanket' or 'open' certificate);
- the name of the policyholder;
- the effective commencement date of the insurance;
- the expiry date of the insurance;
- the persons or classes of persons entitled to drive;
- the limitations on the use of the vehicle.

The certificate carries a statement from the authorised insurers that the policy meets the relevant law in Great Britain, Northern Ireland, the Isle of Man, the Island of Guernsey, the Island of Jersey and the Island of Alderney.

A policy of motor insurance is not valid until a certificate of insurance in the prescribed form has been delivered to the policyholder. Posting is generally taken to constitute delivery and currently, within the context of direct insurance where all aspects of arranging cover are dealt with by telephone, a verbal confirmation of cover is also viewed as delivery (until such time as the courts need to consider the matter, when they may decide otherwise).

If the policy is cancelled after a certificate has been delivered, then the person to whom the certificate was delivered must either surrender the certificate to the company which issued it, or sign a statutory declaration that it has been lost or destroyed.

It is a criminal offence to backdate cover on certificates, to drive without a valid certificate of insurance or to retain a certificate after a policy has been cancelled.

Employer's liability certificate

Certificates of insurance are also required by law for EMPLOYER'S LIABILITY INSURANCE, which was itself made compulsory by the Employer's Liability (Compulsory Insurance) Act 1969.

The form of the certificate is similar to that of the motor insurance certificate, the information required being:

- the name of the policyholder;
- the effective commencement date of the insurance;
- the effective expiry date of the insurance.

As in motor insurance, the certificate carries a statement from the authorised insurers that the policy meets the relevant law in the United Kingdom.

Warning

A certificate of employer's liability insurance must be displayed at each of the employer's business premises.

Claims

Introduction

The process of making a claim will, more than anything else, influence the insured's perception of the quality of service provided by an insurer.

The insurer wishes to provide the cover promised in the policy, but it does not want to exceed its obligations. The insured wants recompense for his or her loss. Between them, they must negotiate a settlement that meets both of these needs.

Notification of claim

Policies carry a condition which requires the insured to notify the insurer as soon as reasonably possible of any incident that might give rise to a claim. In some circumstances, such as theft or malicious damage, the policy may also require the insured to notify the police authorities.

Insurers require early notification so that they can take any necessary action to mitigate the financial consequences of a loss. In the event of a fire, for example, the insurer could immediately appoint a LOSS ADJUSTER who would help the insured in protecting the premises and stock from further damage and in arranging alternative business accommodation whilst repairs or reinstatement take place.

It is good practice to notify insurers in writing of any potential claims as soon as possible, even before completion of a claim form if this is likely to involve some delay, as this will enable them to take early steps to mitigate any loss.

Checklist: Claims terminology

Ex gratia: payment made by the insurer as a gesture of goodwill, **not** as an admission of liability under the policy.

Repudiate: deny the existence of liability under the contract.

Salvage: property saved from destruction by an insured peril.

Void ab initio: deny that the contract ever came into effect.

Without prejudice: cannot subsequently be taken into account in a legal process.

Claim forms

Claim forms are commonly used by insurers to find out about the loss. As notification of the claim, the insured is required to complete a form which is structured to elicit all or most of the information that the insurer needs in order to determine whether policy cover applies and to estimate the extent of the loss.

There are benefits in devising in-house claim forms, if they are organised in a way that makes information readily available to the company and the insurer. This may also encourage the swift completion of forms by employees. Always obtain the insurer's permission before submitting your own claim form – years of development have usually gone into claim forms so that exactly the right information is elicited. Agreeing a format in advance of any need for a claim form is the most effective strategy.

In motor insurance, such forms are known as accident report forms, as the insured is required to report any accident to the insurer, even if no claim is to be made.

Other classes of insurance, such as commercial property covers, would employ the services of a loss adjuster to prepare a detailed report on all aspects of the loss.

Other duties of the insured

Aside from notifying the insurer, common law requires the insured to:

- take whatever reasonable action possible to minimise the loss;
- advise appropriate authorities;
- take all possible steps to prevent a loss from spreading to other property or premises;
- not hinder the insurer in its investigation of the claim.

Failure to comply with these duties may make the claim invalid.

The inclusion of a 'claims procedure' or 'action by insured' condition in the policy makes these duties express rather than implied and gives the insurer the right to repudiate (reject) the claim in the event of any part of the condition being breached.

Checklist: Claim investigation

The insurer will look carefully at the information available about any claim in order to establish key criteria:

- cover was in force at the time of the loss;
- the insured is the insured named in the policy;

- the peril is covered by the policy;
- the insured has done all that is reasonably possible to minimise the loss;
- the insured has complied with the policy conditions;
- there are no applicable exclusions;
- the value of the loss is reasonable.

Although the information sought for different types of claims will vary, the purpose of seeking the information is to enable the insurer to check these points.

Valid and invalid claims

If the insured has disclosed fully and truthfully all the necessary information about the risk at inception, has paid the necessary premium and fulfilled all the requirements of the policy conditions and any warranties, a claim will be valid if it also meets the key criteria above.

In the event of fraud, or breach of a condition or warranty, or the failure of the claim to meet one of these criteria, it will be invalid.

The insurer may repudiate such a claim (i.e. refute its validity) or declare the policy void if there was fraud at its inception (see CONTRACT OF INSURANCE). If the policy is declared void then no contract has existed and premiums must be returned to the insured. If a policy is current but a claim does not fall within the terms of the cover that it provides, no refund of premiums is made, as the cover has still been provided during the period of insurance up to the claim and will continue to be provided until the end of the period of insurance.

Measurement of loss

It is the insured's responsibility to prove to the insurer's satisfaction that a financial loss has occurred and, in most claims relating to general insurance, to quantify the loss and prove that figure.

In liability insurances, the amount of the loss (quantum) will be the amount awarded by a court in damages. In life assurance and other agreed value general insurances, the amount to be claimed is that agreed at policy inception. For life assurance, proof of loss would generally be a copy of the death certificate.

Claim settlement

Claims can be settled by monetary payment, by repair, replacement or reinstatement (see INDEMNITY). The method of settlement available to the insurer is specified in the policy.

The amount of a settlement can be reduced if AVERAGE applies, if there are any EXCESSES applicable to the policy, or if a contribution is required from the insured in respect of betterment (see INDEMNITY).

The sum insured is the maximum amount payable under a property policy; referred to as the sum assured in respect of a life policy. The limit of liability is the maximum payment possible under a liability policy.

If a claim is large, a loss adjuster may assist in the settlement negotiations.

Disputes

If a dispute about the amount to be paid under a policy cannot otherwise be resolved, the dispute can be referred to arbitration in line with the policy condition to this effect or, in the case of personal insurances, referred to the INSURANCE OMBUDSMAN BUREAU.

Legal action is the final recourse for the resolution of a dispute, but few disputes need to be resolved in this way.

Checklist: Making effective claims

- Complete claim forms accurately and truthfully.
- Keep receipts, copy invoices or any other documentation that will help to establish actual valuations of insured property.
- Notify insurers as soon as possible about actual or potential claims.
- Take all steps within your power to minimise the loss.
- Establish if there are any witnesses to the incident (e.g. an employer's liability claim) who can provide independent information.
- Report any incidents to the relevant authorities (e.g. theft to the police and obtain a crime number).
- Pass on to insurers immediately any correspondence from third parties relating to the claim.
- Comply with the claims conditions in the policy.
- Provide all of the information that the insurer requests.
- Provide access to the insurer's representatives as requested.
- For large losses, consider appointing a loss assessor to help negotiate the claim, but agree the fee before confirming the appointment.

Combined and package policies

Introduction

The idea of putting together different types of covers in a single contract arose from insurers' desire to reduce both their own and their clients' administration costs.

Although combined and package policies both gather together different insurances under one contract, there are significant differences in the way that they are structured and operate.

Combined policies

These provide cover under a single contract for all those risks that a small business may encounter. In the absence of combined policies, individual policies would be needed for:

- BUSINESS INTERRUPTION INSURANCE;
- EMPLOYER'S LIABILITY INSURANCE;
- FIRE AND SPECIAL PERILS INSURANCE;
- GLASS INSURANCE;
- THEFT INSURANCE.

The proposer completes one proposal form which deals with all the necessary information and pays one premium. However, the insurer deals with all of the different covers as if they were separate policies, underwriting, rating and applying terms, conditions and warranties individually.

This means that the insured must comply with the requirements of each of the individual policies under the single 'umbrella'. A breach of a warranty for a liability policy section would not therefore be likely to invalidate cover under the fire policy section. However, if the insured did not comply with a condition that applied to all sections of the policy, then the whole policy would be affected.

A limit is normally imposed on the sum insured and larger businesses may find that this limit does not accommodate their needs, which would be better met by separate policies. A large loss in one of the policy sections could exhaust the amount available for losses under the other section.

Insurers encourage businesses to take out cover under a number of sections by offering discounts for multiple section use. They do this to remove the anti-selection risk that would otherwise exist, with businesses choosing to insure only those aspects of their activities with which they anticipate there being problems.

Package policies

Whereas combined policies are essentially one policy acting as an umbrella for several other individual policies operating independently, a package policy is a genuine combination of cover, with one set of conditions, terms and warranties applicable to the whole policy. This makes the package policy much simpler to understand and to operate.

Checklist: Policy cover

The policy offers the full range of commercial covers:

- employer's liability;
- public liability;
- products liability;
- goods in transit;
- theft;
- money;
- glass;
- fire;
- material damage;
- consequential loss (business interruption);
- fidelity guarantee (some include this).

One proposal form provides the underwriter with information on all these risks. The policy will be subject to built-in limits of indemnity and restrictions on cover because of its need to provide cover for a range of perils.

The main rating factor is the district in which the insured business is located, with a rate being applied to the sum insured.

Package policies are also suitable for smaller businesses where the values at risk are fairly low and where sophisticated assessment of the risk and individualised cover are not important.

Compulsory insurance

Introduction

Insurance can be made compulsory by statute, through membership of a professional association or by contract.

Legislation to make a form of insurance compulsory is usually introduced as a result of national concern that compensation be available for those injured, or whose property is damaged, or who suffer some other form of loss as a result of someone else's negligence. By requiring people whose actions may give rise to such a liability to take out insurance, the financial burden of providing compensation can be moved from the state to the private sector.

The two main forms of compulsory insurance are MOTOR INSURANCE and EMPLOYER'S LIABILITY INSURANCE, considered in some detail in specific entries. In addition, the following forms of insurance are compulsory.

Dangerous wild animals/dangerous dogs

Those who own dangerous animals, as defined by the Dangerous Wild Animals Act 1976 or the Dangerous Dogs Act 1991, are required to take out insurance in respect of their liability for injury, loss or damage caused by their animal(s).

Neither statute defines the type or scope of the insurance that must be effected, leaving this to the judgement of the local authority issuing the certificate permitting ownership of the animal. Insurers usually add this cover to an existing contract such as household contents, rather than issuing specific policies, as their exposure would otherwise be unacceptably high.

Riding establishments

Proprietors of riding establishments must take out PUBLIC LIABILITY INSURANCE to cover their liability for injuries to people riding the establishment's horses, or to members of the public. The policy must also provide cover for the horse riders against any injury to members of the public arising from the hire or use of the horses. The requirement for insurance is set out in the Riding Establishments Act 1970, although the statute does not say what scope the insurance should have.

Solicitors

The Solicitors (Amendment) Act 1974 requires solicitors to hold PROFESSIONAL INDEMNITY INSURANCE. The Act specifies that the insurance must cover any claims for financial loss which a client has suffered through the negligence of the solicitor.

Insurance brokers

The Insurance Brokers (Registration) Act 1977 requires all registered insurance brokers (see INTERMEDIARIES) to take out professional indemnity insurance, covering their liability in respect of financial loss caused by their negligence. The cover must apply up to a limit of £250,000, or three times the value of the brokerage on the business, whichever produces the higher figure.

Professional indemnity

Some professional bodies require their members to take out PROFESSIONAL INDEMNITY INSURANCE. The Royal Institution of Chartered Surveyors is one such body.

Contractual requirement to insure

It is common for contracts to require the contractor to take out some form of insurance. Standard forms of contract, e.g. the Joint Contract Tribunal clauses, specify the person responsible for arranging required insurances and what indemnity should be provided. The Royal Institute of British Architects draws up standard forms of contract with clauses identifying what insurance must be arranged.

Nuclear establishments

It is compulsory for nuclear establishments to effect PUBLIC LIABILITY INSURANCE and material damage insurance (see BUSINESS INTERRUPTION INSURANCE). Cover is provided by the British Insurance (Atomic Energy) Committee. Major installations must have cover in excess of £140 million, smaller installations in excess of £10 million.

Conditions

Introduction

Conditions form an essential part of the CONTRACT OF INSURANCE.

Contract terms may be expressed as conditions, as exclusions or as warranties, and sometimes the word 'condition' can be used to describe any of these.

A condition usually places a requirement upon a party to the contract to do something (or not to do something) in a particular situation.

There are three types of conditions in insurance policies, those which are:

- precedent to the contract;

- subsequent to the contract;

- precedent to liability.

Conditions precedent to the contract

If a condition is precedent to the contract, this means that breach of the condition will result in the whole contract becoming void. In this respect it is similar to a WARRANTY, although whereas breach of a warranty automatically avoids the contract, breach of a condition precedent to the contract may have to be shown to have led to the loss before the contract may be avoided. Conditions precedent to the contract are usually implied conditions (see CONTRACT OF INSURANCE).

Conditions subsequent to the contract

Once the contract is in force, these conditions must be complied with for cover to continue. An example would be that the insurer must be notified immediately about any alteration to the risk.

Conditions precedent to liability

Breach of a condition precedent to liability can result in liability for a particular loss being repudiated, but not in the whole contract being avoided, so that a later claim could be paid in full if it was not related to the original breach.

General conditions

These conditions are found in most non-life insurance policies. They set out what each of the parties to the contract must do in specific circumstances.

Checklist: General conditions

The general conditions specify that:

- the insurer must be told of any potential claim as soon as possible (notification);
- liability should not be admitted or denied, or the claim negotiated, without the insurer's permission (conduct of claims);
- the insurer may defend or settle any legal actions against the insured and take over the insured's rights to recover damages from a responsible third party (SUBROGATION);
- where property is insured the policyholder must keep it in a good state of repair (maintenance);
- if the insured has more than one policy covering the same risk then each insurer will only pay that proportion of a claim which relates to their share of the risk (CONTRIBUTION);
- an arbitrator will settle any disputes about the amount to be paid in settlement of a claim (arbitration);
- the insurer must be told as soon as possible about any changes to the risk (alteration);
- the policy can be cancelled by the insured writing to the insurer or by the insurer giving seven days' notice to the insured by recorded delivery to the address on the latest schedule (cancellation).

Other conditions

Some commercial insurance policies include conditions that relate to AVERAGE and to reinstatement (see INDEMNITY).

The policy

The conditions are always set out in the policy. It is increasingly common for policies to be written in plain English, which makes them much easier to understand.

Contract conditions

Introduction

Where contractors and subcontractors work for a principal, their work is usually subject to a contract. Particular trades, especially those related to construction, have developed standard forms of contract, incorporating clauses agreed by the interested parties.

Amongst other things, these contracts set out where the duty to insure rests between the principal, contractor and subcontractor in different circumstances.

This is an extremely complex area and beyond the scope of this guide. Summarised below are the main standard contracts.

Standard form of building contract

This is issued by the Joint Contracts Tribunal. The following clauses relate to insurance:

- clauses 20.1 and 20.2 deal with the contractor's liability to indemnify his principal in the event of injury to a person or damage to property;
- clause 21 imposes a requirement on the contractor to take out and maintain insurance against injury to persons and damage to property;
- clause 21.2.1 requires the contractor on the request of the architect to effect a Joint Names policy to cover nuisance risks;
- clause 22 relates to the insurances that must be effected to cover the works.

Institute of Civil Engineers Conditions of Contract

The following clauses relate to insurance:

- clause 21 specifies that all risks insurance must be effected on the contract works;
- clause 22 requires the contractor to indemnify the principal against injury to persons and damage to property;

- clause 23 requires insurance to be effected to cover the liabilities in respect of bodily injury and property damage;
- clause 24 excludes the principal from liability to the employees of the contractor for employer's liability risks;
- clause 25 requires the contractor to produce evidence to show that the required insurances are in place;
- clause 29 requires the contractor to indemnify the principal against liabilities in respect of interference with traffic, access to properties, noise and pollution.

Construction Plant Hire Association (CPHA) Model Conditions

The clauses below relate to insurance:

- clause 8 states that if a driver is supplied with plant then he must be competent and will be under the direction and control of the hirer;
- clause 13 sets out the hirer's responsibility for loss and damage.

General Conditions of Contract for Building and Civil Engineering

These government contracts stipulate the following:

- condition 8 requires insurance to be effected for the duration of the contract for employer's liability, loss or damage to the works and personal injury or loss or damage to property arising in connection with the works;
- condition 19 relates to loss and damage and requires the contractor to reimburse the local authority for loss, damage, costs and expenses.

General Conditions of Contract for Erection and Installation of Electrical and Mechanical Plant

These are recommended by the Institute of Mechanical Engineers, the Institution of Electrical Engineers and the Association of Consulting Engineers and are usually referred to as IMechE or IEE conditions:

- clauses 43.2 to 43.6 identify who must indemnify whom in what circumstances;
- clauses 47.1, 47.4 and 47.5 impose insuring requirements on various parties.

Goods in transit

The Road Haulage Association has Standard Conditions for the Carriage of Goods, which limit its liability to £1,300 per metric tonne.

Similarly, the Freight Transport Association issues Model Conditions of Carriage which limit its liability to £2,000 per metric tonne or £500 per total consignment, whichever is the greater figure.

Contribution

Introduction

Contribution, a central principle of insurance, operates to ensure that an insured does not receive more than INDEMNITY in respect of a loss. If the purpose of indemnity is to restore the insured to the financial position enjoyed before the loss, then permitting the insured to profit from a loss would defeat this principle. Contribution is a consequence of indemnity, as is SUBROGATION.

When contribution operates

Where at least two indemnity policies cover a common interest, subject-matter and peril (see PROXIMATE CAUSE), and become liable for a loss, each insurer will contribute a proportion of the claim.

The conditions that must be met for contribution to exist do not specify that exactly the same peril, subject-matter and interest be covered by the policies, only that there must be an overlap between the policies.

If two people jointly own property that would constitute common interest, but the different interests of an owner and a bailee would not. Common subject-matter is likely usually to be property, but could be a liability, and the meaning of a common peril is clear.

Common law

The common law position on contribution is that an insured may choose to claim from any liable insurer. This insurer, if the claim is valid, must pay it to the limit of its liability and can only seek contribution from other policies after the claim has been paid. (This remains true for marine policies.)

Contribution condition

Insurers would prefer not to have to pay the whole claim and then call upon others to contribute and negotiate the recovery of the appropriate amounts.

Consequently, most non-marine insurance policies carry a contribution condition, which states that the insurer will contribute only its rateable proportion of any loss to which contribution applies. This then places the responsibility of recovering the rest of the loss on the insured, who will choose whether to claim on the other policies.

Non-contribution clauses

Some policies carry clauses which state that the policy will not apply if the insured is entitled to indemnity under any other insurance. If two such policies were held, theoretically the insured would be precluded from making any recovery. A court would be unlikely to uphold such a situation and in practice both policies would contribute their rateable proportion.

Employer's liability and motor claims

In the event of a road traffic accident in which a passenger travelling in the course of his or her employment is injured, the motor insurer would settle the claim. Changes to the Motor Vehicles Regulations and to the Employer's Liability Regulations have resulted in this agreement.

Market agreements

The rules of the Fire Offices Committee (now part of the ASSOCIATION OF BRITISH INSURERS) modify the usual conditions under which contribution applies, by requiring contribution even where the policies cover different interests.

This will in some instances avoid the need for one insurer to sue another to obtain a full recovery and in others prevent the loss being reimbursed twice over. There are restrictions on these rules, which will not apply, for example, to property outside Great Britain, to consequential loss or public liability policies, to employees' property or tenants' interests or within financial limits.

Lloyd's of London and the ABI have agreed that any claims in respect of property covered by a household contents policy and also by the personal effects section of a motor policy will be settled in full by the insurer to whom the claim is notified, with no recourse to contribution.

Basis of contribution

Once it has been agreed that policies will contribute, the proportion due from each must be established. Two main methods are used: sum insured and independent liability.

Sum insured

The loss is shared in proportion to the sums insured involved. This method commonly applies to property policies covering identical subject-matter.
   The formula is:

$$\frac{\text{sum insured}}{\text{total sum insured on all policies}} \quad \text{x} \quad \text{loss}$$

Case study

Taking two policies with sums insured of £20,000 and £40,000 and a loss of £30,000 gives the calculation:

Policy 1 $\dfrac{20,000}{60,000}$ x 30,000 = £10,000

Policy 2 $\dfrac{40,000}{60,000}$ x 30,000 = £20,000

Independent liability

This method determines contribution by calculating the liability of each insurer separately, as if it was the only provider of cover. It is used more commonly for commercial property insurances where AVERAGE applies, where the sum insured is subject to a loss limit, or in liability insurances.
   The formula for calculating contribution in this way is:

$$\frac{\text{sum insured}}{\text{total value at risk}} \quad \text{x} \quad \text{loss}$$

Case study

If we take the same figures as above, and assume a total value at risk of £60,000, then the calculations would be the same. However, if the insured had underinsured the risk, and the total value at risk was, say, £80,000, then the results would differ:

Policy 1 $\dfrac{20,000}{80,000} \times 30,000 = 8,500$

Policy 2 $\dfrac{40,000}{80,000} \times 30,000 = 15,000$

Because of the underinsurance the contribution from both insurers would be £22,500, leaving the insured to bear the proportion of the loss related to the amount of underinsurance, some £7,500.

If the insurers' total liability is less than, or equal to, the loss, they contribute in proportion to their independent liabilities:

Policy 1 $\dfrac{10,000 \text{ (10,000 maximum)}}{25,000} \times 30,000 = 12,000$

Policy 2 $\dfrac{15,000 \text{ (15,000 maximum)}}{25,000} \times 30,000 = 18,000$

If, on the other hand, the total liability exceeds the loss then the loss will be split in proportion to the independent liabilities, according to the formula:

$$\dfrac{\text{insurer's independent liability}}{\text{total of all insurers' independent liabilities}} \quad \times \quad \text{loss}$$

Policy 1 $\dfrac{10,000}{25,000} \times 20,000 = 8,000$

Policy 2 $\dfrac{15,000}{25,000} \times 20,000 = 12,000$

Cover notes

Introduction

The policy document provides evidence of the existence of an insurance contract, but policies and other documents such as certificates and schedules take some time to issue. In many types of insurance this delay does not matter, but in some cases it is necessary to be able to demonstrate that cover is in force. This applies particularly to compulsory insurance.

In such cases, a cover note is issued, normally by the agent through whom cover is arranged, but sometimes by the insurer itself, so that the policyholder can prove that he or she has insurance. The cover note contains brief details of the cover and a confirmation that the policyholder is insured.

Motor insurance

A motor insurance cover note acts as a temporary policy document and temporary certificate of insurance and therefore contains more information than an actual certificate would contain.

Cover notes may not be backdated – to do so is a criminal offence. Any break in cover would result in the insured driving without insurance. Because cover may not be backdated, the permanent certificate issued after a break in cover must start from the date when the subsequent period of continuous cover began.

Warning

It is essential to obtain a new cover note before the expiry of the old one if permanent policy documents have not yet been issued.

Credit insurance

Introduction

Few commercial organisations could survive without using some form of credit, which is the practice of buying or selling goods without payment being made immediately. As payment is deferred until a later date, there is a risk that at that later date, the seller will be left without remuneration. This risk is what is insured by credit insurance, which relates to the provision of goods and services. It provides indemnity for the seller of goods in the event of the buyer of goods failing to pay for those goods delivered on credit terms.

Extent of cover

In order to encourage the insured business to exercise caution in the choice of persons to whom it extends credit, and to do as much as possible to recover payment, in most cases policies will cover up to 80% or 90% of a loss, but seldom the full amount.

Similarly, credit insurance does not cover loss of profits, only the insured's actual financial interest in the goods. A manufacturer's or retailer's mark-up for profit will remain uninsured. It is up to the underwriter to decide the percentage of the credit risk that can be insured and at what rate.

Types of cover

The usual trading relationship between a manufacturer or retailer and customers, either in the UK or overseas, will be covered by a domestic credit insurance policy, although catastrophe cover for companies needing protection against major bad debt losses and cover to protect companies against the political risks of exporting goods overseas is also available.

Domestic credit cover

Domestic credit cover can be written in a number of ways, listed below.

Whole turnover policy

This is the usual method of insuring credit risks, taking the entire credit risk of an organisation into consideration, so that areas where performance has been better than average compensate for poor areas and enable a rate to be quoted on the average performance.

The premium rate quoted will be influenced by the length of credit term offered by the company, the mixture of risk between large and small accounts, the company's own loss record and the insurer's opinion about the credit record of the company's clients.

When a premium rate has been determined, it will usually be applied to each £100 of turnover, with a maximum limit of indemnity of 80% to 85% of losses. A discretionary limit is agreed and the company can offer credit up to this limit to customers after having made its own enquiries without having to confer with the insurer. If the company wants to offer credit of more than the limit, then before doing so it must confirm with the insurer that this is acceptable.

This is the only type of cover that protects the insured's whole account. If the insured has particular concerns about specific accounts only then the covers below offer the chance to be more selective. However, unexpected losses on the rest of the account would not be covered and premiums may be higher because of the extent to which the insurer is being selected against, i.e. being asked to cover risks on which it is more likely that claims will be made.

Principal customer policy

Premium is based on turnover, but turnover only from the organisations that the company identifies as its principal customers. The limit of indemnity is likely to be 85% to 90%.

Specific account policy

If the company is concerned about the credit risk from particular clients, it can arrange a policy just to cover that risk, although insurers are less likely to offer this cover as it is far more likely that a claim will be made against the policy.

Insurers will set premium rates and limits of indemnity (probably as low as 75%) after conducting enquiries into the credit rating of the customer.

Single contract cover

This operates in a similar way to the specific account policy, but just for one contract, rated on the value of the contract with similar indemnity limits imposed.

Catastrophe cover

This is appropriate if a company wants to protect itself against an unexpected catastrophe, but is confident about its day-to-day credit control systems.

A qualifying limit is set by the insurer, with only bad debts above this limit being covered, usually for 100% indemnity. However, a deductible (large excess) is usually imposed on qualifying losses to encourage the insured to take care to minimise such losses. The policy will also be subject to a maximum limit of liability, reflecting the extent and spread of risk. A single premium is paid at inception of each policy term.

Political cover

Because political risks are better assessed and covered by government agencies than by private insurers, the Export Credit Guarantee Department (ECGD) was set up to issue policies which cover UK exporters against loss from the commercial failure of overseas buyers or from payment being frustrated for political or economic reasons.

Cover is provided for:

- failure to honour obligations to pay under letters of credit;
- losses when foreign exchange is prevented from being paid;
- repudiation of contracts;
- confiscation of plant or equity overseas;
- losses arising from non-delivery by a foreign country for political reasons.

Export credit cover

This constitutes an all-in-one package covering commercial and political risks for companies who rely extensively on exporting their goods or services, and includes:

- whole turnover cover;
- political risks;
- confiscation;
- unfairly requiring payment under contractual bonds.

Critical illness insurance

Introduction

Critical illness insurance (formerly known as 'dread disease' insurance) recognises that in the event of a person being diagnosed as having a critical illness, they may well face financial difficulties. It therefore pays out the agreed sum assured on the insured being diagnosed as suffering from certain specified illnesses or conditions. There is no payment on death, just on diagnosis to meet immediate financial needs – life assurance would still be needed to provide funds for the insured's dependants in the event of his or her death.

Cover

Some policies may provide cover for up to 30 conditions, but the most commonly covered are:

- cancer;
- stroke;
- coronary heart disease;
- heart attack;
- kidney failure;
- major organ transplant.

Cover is usually written on a single or joint life basis, for a capital sum, likely to be between £100,000 and £1 million plus.

Extensions

It is possible for the policy to include an increasability option without need for evidence of health within certain limits. This means that the sum insured could be increased at a later date without the insured needing to prove that he or she was still in good health. Benefits can also be index-linked to ensure that their value remains the same rather than being eroded by inflation.

Underwriting considerations

In determining whether or not to accept the risk and considering the premium rate and any terms to be applied, the underwriter will look at:

- the applicant's age, health and family medical history;
- the capital sum payable;
- whether index-linking of benefits or increasability option is to be included.

Directors' and officers' liability

Introduction

Any director of a company can incur a personal liability through failure to discharge his or her specific duties and responsibilities properly. As the directors represent the will of the company, they can incur a civil or criminal liability for any wrong done by the company.

Common law liability

At common law, directors can become liable as a result of a lack of care and skill shown in the performance of their duties. There is a duty upon directors that they should act honestly and in good faith and carry out their duties with reasonable care and whatever skills they possess.

In *Re City Equitable Fire Insurance Co.* (1925) it was stated that: 'A director need not exhibit in the performance of his duties a greater degree of skill than may reasonably be expected from a person of his knowledge and experience.'

The common law duty of care has increased over the years and a full-time director today would be expected to have a thorough knowledge of the company's activities.

Statutory liability

Section 214 of the Insolvency Act 1986 allows the liquidator of an insolvent company to seek a personal contribution from any director who knew that insolvency was a likely outcome and yet allowed the company to continue to trade to the detriment of its creditors. Prior to 1986 a director could only be held personally liable if fraud could be proven.

In addition to the personal contribution, such a director may be disqualified from being a director or a manager of a company for up to 15 years, under section 10 of the Company Directors Disqualification Act 1986.

Criminal proceedings may be taken against any director under the Health and Safety at Work etc. Act 1974 where an offence committed by a company can be proved to have been committed with the consent and connivance of a director or person acting in such a capacity, or attributable to any neglect on his or her part.

The Environmental Protection Act 1990 also makes directors and officers liable for breaches caused through their neglect, consent or contrivance.

Policy cover

Directors' and officers' insurance provides cover for directors who may incur some such liability. Policies can be written in two parts, with the first part confirming that, in the event of the company having to indemnify one of its directors against a liability incurred, the company will receive reimbursement from the insurer; and the second part indemnifying the director directly where the company cannot, or will not, indemnify him or her itself. Alternatively, two complementary policies can provide the same cover.

Ideally, the Articles of Association of the company should be changed to confer on the Board the authority to approve and authorise the directors' and officers' policy, as otherwise authorisation by an officer or director of the company may invalidate cover for that person (since they may have a vested interest in the cover).

Cover is provided for the whole board and for directors of any subsidiary companies. Individual cover can be arranged for a director for all directorships held. This latter would be a contract between the director and the insurer and would in no way involve the companies for which directorships are held.

Policy cover for the company

The policy covers losses arising from claim(s) against directors or officers:

- by reason of a wrongful act in their capacities as directors and officers; or
- arising from an official investigation or other proceedings;
- where the insured is required to indemnify the directors or officers at common law, or under statute, or under the Memorandum and Articles of Association of the insured company.

The policy is written on a claims made basis, which means that claims must be made during the period of insurance for the indemnity to apply.

Definitions

Loss means any amount that the insured company has to pay to a director as indemnity for any wrongful act, and includes awards of damages, legal costs and expenses incurred in defending an action against the director in the courts. It does not include fines, penalties, punitive or exemplary damages awarded against him, as this would be against public policy.

Any actual or alleged breach of trust or of duty, neglect, error, misstatement, misleading statement, omission or other act wrongfully committed, or breach of warranty of authority in the director's performance of his duties, constitutes a wrongful act.

Checklist: Policy exclusions

The policy contains the common market exclusions for liability policies:

* war, riot and civil commotion;
* radioactive contamination;
* pre-existing circumstances known or thought likely to lead to a claim;
* indemnity being available to the insured from another source;
* jurisdiction clauses excluding legal actions in the USA and Canada.

It also excludes those risks insured more specifically under other liability policies:

* libel or slander;
* products liability;
* copyright or patents infringement;
* pollution liability;
* professional indemnity.

Directors' and officers' policies specifically exclude:

* losses from a personal guarantee or warranty given by the director;
* dishonesty, fraud or malicious conduct of the director;
* instances of the director gaining any profit or advantage to which he or she was not entitled;
* arrangements where the director is involved in a capacity other than purely as a director;
* claims from one director against another;
* failure to effect and maintain insurance on behalf of the insured.

Limit of liability

The policy schedule will specify the total limit of liability.

Conditions

Similar to other liability insurance policies:

- immediate notice must be given of any claims;
- insured must cooperate with insurers;
- insured must not take any action to prejudice the insurers (such as admitting liability);
- cancellation provisions are specified;
- policy void if fraudulent claim made.

Additionally, the insured must give his or her consent before a claim can be settled, but if he or she refuses and the claims settlement eventually exceeds the figure at which the insurer would have settled, the insurer is only liable for the lower sum plus costs and expenses incurred up to that time.

If a take-over offer is declared unconditional then only wrongful acts before the take-over is declared unconditional are covered.

Policy cover for the individual

This reflects the cover available for companies, providing an indemnity to the director against loss arising from any claim during the period of the policy by reason of any wrongful act in his or her capacity as director or officer of the company, or arising from an official investigation.

Some policies also provide cover for costs incurred pursuing or defending a claim arising from a director's position as a director, or in defending an action that could result in the director's disqualification from the company.

Definitions

Loss means any sum that the insured becomes legally liable to pay in connection with claims made following any wrongful act. It would include:

- awards of damages and costs;
- legal costs from defending a civil or criminal legal action;
- legal costs for representation at an official investigation.

As with the company policy, fines, penalties, exemplary and punitive damages awards are excluded as against public policy.

Checklist: Risk assessment

Proposal forms are used to elicit all the necessary information and contain questions on the following areas:

- company name, address, and the name of any holding company;
- business activities;
- previous insurances;
- names, ages and positions held of all those who are directors or officers of the company or any subsidiary;
- number of shareholders;
- percentage of shares held by directors;
- shareholdings exceeding 5% of any class of issued shares;
- share listings on stock exchanges;
- businesses bought or sold in past year and those contemplated;
- proposals for acquisitions or mergers;
- previous claims and any incidents that may give rise to claims (important because policies are on claims made basis).

The proposer is asked about the limit of indemnity required (usual minimum £250,000).

Other information sought would include audited accounts for the last two periods, a copy of the directors' indemnity clause from the company's Articles of Association and a copy of any circular letters sent to shareholders in the past two years.

Rating

Once the necessary information is to hand, the underwriter can set a rate for the risk.

The rate will be based on:

- number of directors and officers to be covered;
- trade, company activities, business structure;
- turnover and gross assets;
- the company's financial position;
- the limit of indemnity;
- the location of the company's operations and under which jurisdictions these are likely to fall.

Excesses normally apply, which may be £100 for an individual policy and £2,500 or more for a corporate policy.

Duty of disclosure and material facts

Introduction

When an insurance contract is arranged, each side has very little knowledge of the facts at the other side's disposal. The proposer knows a great deal about the risk, but may know nothing about the way insurance operates, about the scope of cover provided by the particular contract or about the insurer. The insurer has extensive knowledge of these things, but is completely ignorant of the risk itself and of the proposer's attitudes to the risk.

Utmost good faith

Because neither the insured nor the insurer can know all the relevant facts about a proposed risk, insurance contracts are based on the principle of utmost good faith (*uberrima fides*). This means that both parties to the contract have an explicit duty to disclose fully and accurately all facts which are material to the risk, whether or not they are specifically asked about these.

The Marine Insurance Act 1906 provides the current legal definition of what constitutes a material fact: 'Every circumstance is material which would influence the judgement of a prudent insurer in fixing the premium or determining whether he will take the risk.'

Checklist: Disclosure requirements

Facts which must be disclosed

Only those facts which are material at the time of disclosure need be disclosed. There is no requirement to predict future material facts.

As a guideline, facts should be disclosed which:

- relate to internal or external factors that make the risk greater than would ordinarily be expected;
- make the amount of loss greater than would ordinarily be expected;
- relate to previous losses or claims; or to instances where cover has been offered at higher than normal (adverse) terms or has been declined altogether and which relate to other policies held;
- relate to the subject matter of insurance;
- limit the insurer's chance of recovering from liable third parties, such as contractual agreements.

Facts that need not be disclosed

Some facts do not need to be disclosed. These are those facts which:

- everyone is assumed to know, e.g. facts of law or those that are common knowledge;
- lessen the risk (although the proposer may wish to do so);
- are covered by policy conditions;
- have been drawn to the insurer's attention or which a survey should have noted (the insurer is said to be 'put on enquiry' and to waive its right to the full information if the initial reference is not pursued);
- the policyholder doesn't know (the ABI Statements of Insurance Practice require the proposer to confirm that facts are given 'to the best of the proposer's knowledge or belief');
- relate to convictions spent under the Rehabilitation of Offenders Act 1974. (For a minor conviction, after a certain period of time has passed, the proposer may answer questions as if the conviction never existed. Some offences meriting particular sentences can never be spent, e.g. custodial sentences exceeding 30 months.)

Duration of disclosure

The common law position is that the duty of disclosure begins when contract negotiations start and terminates when cover is offered and accepted and the contract is formed. There is then no need to disclose subsequent changes for the duration of the contract.

Policies may sometimes include a condition that requires any changes to the risk during the contract period to be disclosed. Insurers may emphasise their right to decline to underwrite such changes. This requirement can apply just to particular types of facts rather than to any material change to the risk; e.g. a motor policy might insist on any changes of vehicle being notified immediately, but be happy to accept notification of a motoring conviction at next renewal.

At renewal for general insurances (i.e. not long-term contracts) the duty of disclosure revives as if the contract were being completely renegotiated. Insurers cannot alter the renewal terms offered on long-term policies and therefore the duty of disclosure does not revive at renewal.

Employer's liability insurance

Introduction

Employer's liability insurance is compulsory in the United Kingdom. Any policy issued must meet the requirements of the Employer's Liability (Compulsory Insurance) Act 1969 and subsequent Employer's Liability Regulations.

Employer's Liability (Compulsory Insurance) Act 1969

This Act, which took effect on 1 January 1972, requires every employer in Great Britain to take out:

- an approved insurance policy;
- with an authorised insurer;
- against liability for bodily injury or disease;
- sustained by their employees;
- arising out of and in the course of their employment in Great Britain in that business.

Certain family relationships, extending from immediate family to 'step' or 'half' relationships, are exempt from this requirement to insure, as are police and most local authorities.

The Act does not impose any liability on the employer to pay compensation and each case will be determined on its own merits.

Employer's Liability (Compulsory Insurance) General Regulations 1971

These brought the 1969 Act into effect and operate to prohibit insurance policies from containing conditions that would restrict the insurer's liability under the policy.

They also require:

- at least £2* million indemnity to be provided in respect of a claim from any one occurrence involving one or more employees;
- cover to be provided for employees not usually resident in Great Britain but here for over 14 days in the course of their employment;
- a certificate of insurance to be issued within 30 days of policy inception or renewal;
- a certificate of employer's liability insurance to be displayed at all of the insured's business premises;
- the certificate and policy of insurance to be produced for inspection when required.

Employer's Liability (Compulsory Insurance) Exemption Regulations 1971

These list the 23 categories of exempt employers, which are mainly government bodies.

Employer's Liability (Compulsory Insurance) Amendment Regulations 1974

These provide for a certificate of employer's liability insurance to make reference to 'the relevant law' rather than specifying the particular legislation, which differs slightly between different parts of Great Britain.

Employer's Liability (Defective Equipment) Act 1969

This imposed a strict liability (meaning that if the event occurs the employer is liable without the employee needing to prove negligence) on employers for any injuries to employees caused by the use of defective equipment supplied by the employer, even if the employer was unaware of the defect until the injury occurred. The defect must be the fault of a third party (manufacturer or supplier) – if no one is at fault then there is no liability. The employer may try to recoup its payments from the responsible third party. Equipment is defined very widely, and considered to be any article provided by an employer for the purposes of employment.

---

* This figure is likely to increase to £5 million.

Employer's Liability Policy

This provides cover for the employer's liability to compensate an employee for bodily injury or disease arising from their employment.

Cover is for damages payable to the employee and for claimants' costs and expenses.

The actual wording of the policy is: 'indemnity against legal liability for damages and claimants' costs and expenses in respect of bodily injury to or death disease or illness of any person employed caused during any period of insurance, arising out of and in the course of employment by the insured in the business.'

Bodily injury would include nervous shock, but not damage to a person's feelings or reputation.

Employees

A person is an employee if party to a contract of service or apprenticeship with the employer. This is still known as a 'master/servant' relationship and it is important to understand how this relationship can arise, in order to determine for whom liability can be incurred.

If the following criteria are met, then it is likely that a master/servant relationship exists and that liability will be owed to the employee:

- if the employer can select the person to do the work;
- if the person doing the work is paid wages or other remuneration by the employer;
- if the employer can control the method in which the work is done;
- if the employer can suspend or dismiss the person doing the work.

Equally, if the person agrees to use his or her skill to perform a service for the employer in return for remuneration, and agrees that the employer can control the manner in which that service is performed, and the rest of the contract provisions are consistent with a contract of service, then a **contract of service** exists. A further test may be to ask on whose business the person was working – his or her own or the employer's.

Where a person performs certain tasks for a fee, this is a **contract for services** and there is no liability for the person paying for the service.

Most policies cover as employees:

- self-employed persons;
- labour-masters and persons supplied by them;
- those employed by labour – only subcontractors;
- persons hired or borrowed under an agreement that is deemed to represent employment;
- persons on work experience or similar schemes.

Course of employment

To be covered by the employer's liability policy, an injury must arise 'out of and in the course of' a person's employment.

It is difficult to identify exactly what constitutes 'in the course of employment' and a number of legal cases have tried to clarify the situation. The outcomes seem to be:

- If a person enters their employer's premises to work, then from the time they cross the boundary they are acting in the course of their employment.
- If a person is obliged to travel to work in a company vehicle, then they are in the course of their employment, but not if they can choose whether to travel in this or another way.
- If a person is required by their employer to travel from home to a place of work other than their normal place of work, and receives payment from them for that journey then the journey, is in the course of their employment. If the employee chooses to drive his own vehicle to get to that workplace and injures a third party, the employer is vicariously liable for his negligence.

Motor insurance policies have become responsible for liability to persons travelling in the course of their employment following the Third Motor Insurance Directive and the Motor Vehicles (Compulsory Insurance) Regulations 1992, which brought the Directive into effect in the United Kingdom. Employer's liability policies will thus be endorsed so that any risk covered by road traffic act legislation is excluded.

Trade or business

Insurers will confine cover to the trade or business activity on which the premium has been based, but include services ancillary to the insured's business, such as the maintenance of premises or first aid services.

Territorial limits

Policies usually provide cover for Great Britain, Northern Ireland, the Isle of Man or the Channel Islands, or for the vehicle while temporarily outside those territories. If cover is extended to include overseas work, the policy will also include a jurisdiction clause to ensure that any claims are handled on the basis of UK law and damages scales. This is to avoid 'forum shopping', the process by which a claim is placed under whichever jurisdiction related to it makes the highest awards of damages.

Period of insurance

The cause of the bodily injury or disease must happen during the period of insurance. The insurer is liable for such injury or disease even if the policy has lapsed. Actions for personal injuries are usually subject to a time limit of three years, during which an action for damages must be brought. However, because many industrial diseases have no symptoms until years after the damage has been done, the Limitation Acts permit an action to be brought within three years of the affected person knowing about their injury (or discovering other material facts of a decisive nature).

Insurers who have offered cover during the period since when the injury occurred usually agree to share claims proportionately.

Employer's liability cover is known as 'long-tail' business because of the delay in claims being advised and subsequent delay in settlement.

Some insurers may offer retrospective cover on a claims made basis for old risks where policy records may have been destroyed or where policies offered cover which is now inadequate.

Additional cover

Additional cover can apply in respect of:

- contractual liabilities and indemnity to principals;
- claims costs and expenses, costs of legal representation at an inquest or a Court of Summary Jurisdiction;
- indemnity to other persons such as directors, partners or employees of the insured, or the insured's legal personal representatives.

If the insurer has to indemnify the insured because of the compulsory nature of employer's liability insurance, where otherwise it would not have been liable to do so, they may recover (or attempt to do so) the amount of any outlay from the insured.

Limit of indemnity

Initially cover was unlimited, despite the legislative minimum set at £2 million any one occurrence. However, poor claims experience and accumulation risks have led to the application of a common limit of £10 million any one occurrence (including legal fees), although limits above this can be negotiated.

Damage to employee's clothing

This is generally covered if caused at the same time as the bodily injury giving rise to the claim. Otherwise it would fall under the PUBLIC LIABILITY INSURANCE policy.

Injury to feelings

The employer's liability policy is not intended to provide damages for injury to feelings, but if such injury causes mental or emotional distress, then this might be considered bodily injury and thus fall within the cover offered by the policy.

Checklist: Policy extensions, exclusions and conditions

Extensions

The policy may be extended to cover:

- payments to employees if court orders against a negligent third party (not the employer) remain unpaid after six months;
- compensation for court attendance by directors, partners or employees of the insured;
- compensation awarded to an employee following the negligent preparation of references which harm career prospects;
- legal costs and expenses for a director or officer of the insured prosecuted under the Health and Safety at Work etc. Act 1974.

Exclusions

Standard exclusions do not apply to the Employer's Liability policy, because of its compulsory nature: the only exclusion generally applied is illness, injury or disease arising from ionising radiation, radioactive contamination or nuclear explosion.

Conditions

Conditions attached to the policy:

- advice of change of risk: the insurer must be told of any change in the insured's business activities;
- suspension of cover: this enables an insurer to suspend cover if action that has been requested to remove a hazard is not taken within a reasonable time;
- notification of claims: insured must report any incident that may give rise to a claim;
- claims procedures (including subrogation rights): insured gives insurer right to conduct a claim as it thinks best and to take over the insured's rights against a negligent third party;
- reasonable precautions: these must be taken by the insured to prevent accidents and disease and to comply with relevant legislation;

- premium adjustment: if the premium is based on estimated figures the insured must keep accurate records and submit these so that the premium can be adjusted at the end of the period of insurance;
- other insurances: contribution clause;
- cancellation: policy may be cancelled by the insurer sending a registered letter to the insured at their last known address;
- observance of policy conditions: this makes the observance of policy conditions precedent to liability (within the terms of the compulsory insurance legislation).

Proposal form

A combined form is common for employer's liability, public liability and products liability risks.

Questions standard to all classes are:

- proposer's full name;
- proposer's business address;
- trade or business;
- date established;
- previous claims history;
- previous insurances.

The proposal will include a declaration of the answers given being true to the best of the proposer's knowledge and belief.

Checklist: Risk assessment

Questions specific to an employer's liability proposal form:

- schedule of employees, showing numbers and annual remuneration of employees in different categories: clerical staff and non-manual workers; shop assistants; employees using power-driven woodworking machinery; employees using other power-driven machinery; others (described);
- maintenance of plant and premises: whether proper machinery guards and fences are in place, premises in good repair, plant regularly inspected, the Factories Acts and other legislation complied with;
- use of substances hazardous to health: radioactive materials, lasers, silica, asbestos, gases, acids and whether polluting gases etc., are caused by any trade processes;
- noise-induced injuries: do processes involve noise levels above 90dB(A)?

- offshore installations: if work on gas or oil rigs is done, the number of employees involved must be given.

Premiums

Premiums are based on the total annual earnings of all employees engaged in the business and the type of business involved. A rate per mille (‰) is applied to the total wage estimate to reflect the usual risk for the type of trade and is adjusted in respect of the actual claims experience of the proposer.

The initial premium is based on an estimate and is adjusted at the end of the period of insurance when actual earnings are known. The insured must submit a wages adjustment declaration form within 30 days of the expiry of the period of insurance.

If a risk is large enough, a special rate can be worked out on the basis of the past five years' claims experience, rather than by comparison with statistics from similar businesses in the same trade.

Risk classification enables the underwriter to develop standard rates for allied trades rather than starting from new. Classifications range from the most dangerous occupations (mining, quarrying, fisheries, agriculture) to the least dangerous (insurance, banking, finance and business services).

The rating structure takes into account hazards normally associated with a particular trade. If only some of the particular hazards applicable to the trade of the proposer apply to his business, the policy can be endorsed to provide cover only for the risks undertaken and to exclude the others.

Risk surveys

Unusual risks or those with special features are likely to be surveyed by the insurer before cover is offered and a premium rate decided upon. The surveyor will be particularly interested in the physical hazards, but moral hazard (see HAZARD) is also of great significance in this class of business.

Engineering insurance

Introduction

The Factories and Workshops Act 1901 made regular inspection of steam boilers in factories compulsory, a requirement that was later extended to include mines and quarries.

The Health and Safety at Work etc. Act 1974 enforces the duties imposed by earlier legislation and imposes a strict requirement on employers to ensure that all plant and machinery is safe and in a sound working condition. Usually this is interpreted as imposing a minimum requirement of the inspection and maintenance requirements of the individual Acts.

Other legislation increased the demand for inspection services.

Plant and machinery belong to one of three types:

- boilers and pressure plant;

- electrical and mechanical plant;

- lifts, cranes and handling plant.

Inspection service

Engineering insurers provide a regular inspection service by competent engineers throughout the period of insurance, reporting to the insured about the condition of the plant. The main objective of this service is to prevent losses by identifying and remedying faults before they can lead to breakdown.

Inspection also helps plant owners to discharge their obligations under various statutes and is of value where the insured business is too small to justify employing a qualified engineer.

If the plant owner wants engineering cover without the inspection service, or wants just the inspection service and no other cover, insurers are prepared to meet these requirements.

Policy cover

Definitions are provided in the policy for key words such as 'plant', 'explosion', 'collapse' and 'breakdown', so that the same meanings are implied wherever these words appear in the same format in the policy. Most current policies include wide cover for all types of plant within the one wording.

The policy is subject to the limit of indemnity agreed with the insured and specified in the schedule. A typical wording would be:

> The company will indemnify the insured against sudden and unforeseen damage to any plant described in the schedule
>
> - whilst at the situation stated;
> - at any other situation in Great Britain, Northern Ireland, Isle of Man, Channel Islands and the Republic of Ireland at which the plant is temporarily located including transit (other than by sea or by air) between such situations which necessitates repair or replacement of the plant before it can resume normal working.

The cover provided by the phrase 'sudden and unforeseen damage' is wide and essentially cover is provided for anything not specifically excluded. Cover can, however, be limited to only basic explosion, collapse and breakdown.

General exclusions

The policy excludes:

- war, riot, civil commotion;
- ionising radiation or contamination by radioactivity;
- terrorism in Northern Ireland;
- pollution or contamination.

Specific exclusions

Aside from the general exclusions common to most material damage policies, the policy also specifically excludes:

- fire, lightning, explosion (other than that caused by the bursting of insured plant without its contents igniting), earthquake, aircraft or other aerial devices, articles dropped from them, theft, flood or by water discharged or leaking from a sprinkler installation;
- remedying or making good defective seams;

- gradually developing flaws or defects;
- failure of expendable parts;
- damage to non-metallic or decorative surfaces;
- damage caused by erection, dismantling, modification, maintenance or repair.

Extensions

The policy can be extended to include:

- damage to own surrounding property;
- goods being handled or lifted by an insured item of plant;
- explosion of gases in the furnaces or flues of boiler and pressure plant;
- reinstatement of boiler and pressure plant to its condition when new, or to meet the additional cost of complying with building or other regulations to the level required by local authorities when reinstating property destroyed or damaged by explosion or collapse of such plant.

Checklist: Risk assessment

Boiler and pressure plant

Risk assessment will be based on the:

- quality of the building of the plant, whether in accordance with relevant standards;
- presence of required safety devices;
- competence of those responsible for the installation of the plant;
- age of heating boilers (life span 12 to 15 years).

Lifts, cranes and handling plant

Risk assessment will be based on the:

- environment in which they are to operate;
- trade in which they are to engage;
- degree to which they may be operated by unskilled people.

Electrical or mechanical plant

Risk assessment will be based on the:

- age of the plant;
- availability of spare parts;

- environment in which the plant is to operate;
- nature of the manufacturing process if used in factories.

Rating

Premium rates in engineering insurance are based on the capacity for work of the plant involved. Capacities are usually expressed in technical terms, some of the more common are:

- boilers: evaporative capacity – the number of pounds of water that a boiler can evaporate into steam in one hour;
- heating boilers: British thermal units (one BTU is the amount of heat needed to raise the temperature of one pound of water by one degree Fahrenheit);
- electrical plant: kilowatts (kW) or kilovoltamps (kVA), or these figures converted into horsepower.

Inspection charges take up a large proportion of any premium received and therefore the choice of inspection frequency is an important factor in deciding upon the appropriate premium levels.

Stand-by plant that is used only in the event of a failure of a main piece of machinery can be insured at a very reduced rate because of the reduced risk.

Excesses are common to engineering insurance, varying from £50 to £1,000 plus, depending on the type of cover being provided.

Limits of indemnity

A single accident limit usually now applies to all plant at one location.

Works machinery policies

These have developed in response to requests for as wide a form of cover as possible. They provide cover for all plant and machinery used in factories, against a variety of risks. Large excesses apply to this form of cover. The inspection service may be provided as part of a separate contract.

Cover provided is typically:

- sudden and unforeseen damage to all plant while the plant is
  (i) working or at rest;
  (ii) being dismantled, moved or re-erected in another position at the situation stated in the schedule;

- damage to property belonging to the insured or for which he is responsible;
- liability for hired-in plant.

The policy may exclude damage to:

- computers and data processing equipment;
- office equipment;
- communication or alarm systems.

The policy contains a declaration clause under which the insured advises the insurer of the value of the plant at each renewal, and the premium is arrived at by applying a percentage rate to this value.

These are often known as trade risk policies, with the basic rate (per cent or per mille) depending on the type of the trade. The insurer will decide how frequent inspections need to be in order to control the risk and specify that all statutory examinations must be made by a competent person.

Other risks

Engineering insurers can also provide the following forms of cover:

- works damage insurance: covers loss/damage to machinery and plant by accidents during the manufacturing process;
- deterioration of stock: in cold stores from failure of public electricity supplies, breakdown, accident or the effect of escaped refrigerant fumes;
- computer insurance: material damage to installation and financial costs on losses incurred as a direct result of material damage to the installation;
- machinery movement: loss or damage in transit, dismantling or erecting, positioning, resiting, lifting/lowering, testing/commissioning;
- machinery business interruption: (see BUSINESS INTERRUPTION INSURANCE) insures losses arising from material damage to plant other than from fire or special perils;
- hired-in plant: protection against any liability assumed by the hirer of plant under the terms of an agreement to compensate for loss or damage to the machine in his custody or control; breakdown through hirer's negligence or misuse; continuing hire charges following such loss; legal expenses in defence of legal proceedings;
- extraneous damage: accidental damage external in origin and unrelated to any defect in machinery itself covered (not fire, lightning, theft, breakdown/explosion, replaceable parts or gradual deterioration).

Estimated maximum loss

Introduction

An insurer will want to assess the extent of its possible exposure once it has accepted a risk, mainly to determine how much of the risk will be retained for its own account and how much reinsured.

Assessing EML

An insurer will try to calculate four different figures:

- the total sum insured (TSI), which is the total of all values at risk at all sites;
- the estimated amount at risk (EAR), which is likely to be the total sum insured at any one location;
- the estimated maximum loss (EML), an estimate of the worst effect that the operation of an insured peril could have in any one location;
- the estimated maximum probable loss (EMPL), an estimate of the likely result of the operation of an insured peril.

Case study

A large manufacturing company could have five different manufacturing sites in five different locations. Let's assume that the values at risk are:

1. £50,000

2. £130,000

3. £100,000

4. £80,000

5. £200,000

If the company takes out fire insurance to cover all of its sites, the **total sum insured** will be £560,000.

For Site 3, the **estimated amount at risk** would be £100,000.

The **estimated maximum loss,** if all facilities on the site were completely destroyed by fire, is the same figure.

However, in assessing the **estimated maximum probable loss** the insurer would take into account factors such as fire-resistant construction, sprinkler systems and fire alarms. It may therefore conclude that because of these factors and the distance between buildings on the site, it is unlikely that more than two would be destroyed at any one time. The EMPL would therefore be the value of the two buildings, which would be less than the EML.

ABI definition

The ASSOCIATION OF BRITISH INSURERS has issued a recommended definition of estimated maximum loss:

An estimation of the maximum loss which could reasonably be sustained from the contingencies under consideration, as a result of an incident considered to be within the realms of probability taking into account all factors likely to increase or lessen the extent of the loss, but excluding such coincidences and catastrophes which may be possible but remain unlikely.

Checklist: Calculating EML

In calculating the EML for a fire risk, six main factors would be considered:

- values involved and how the risk is divided;
- the construction of the property;
- the insured's occupation;
- how combustible and prone to damage the contents are;
- fire protection systems and appliances;
- management and housekeeping standards.

The insurer's conclusions about the EML would then be used to determine the amount to be held within its own account and the amount of the risk to be reinsured.

A similar process of assessing risk factors would be used for whatever type of insurance cover applied.

Excesses, deductibles, franchises

Introduction

Insurers often offer reductions in premium if the insured is willing to carry some of the cost of any claim.

Excesses and deductibles

If the insured agrees to fund the first amount of each and every claim, that amount is known as an excess.

Excesses are common in private motor insurance and other personal lines. In return for agreeing to pay the first £50 or £100 of a claim an insured could attract a significant premium discount. A commercial motor fleet might choose to operate a £500 excess on its policy, so that the claims experience of the entire fleet was not adversely affected by lots of small claims. If a vehicle was involved in a minor accident, falling within the excess, the fleet owner would settle the claim itself and only have recourse to the policy for more significant claims.

Excesses may be imposed for some types of cover, e.g. a young driver on a motor policy may only be allowed to drive the vehicle if a £250 excess applies to any claims that arise through his or her use of it. Equally, in buildings insurance, an excess may be imposed for storm or flood cover. In these instances, insurers are trying to encourage policyholders to take particular care by making them share in the risk.

Excesses are slightly at odds with the principle of indemnity which requires the policyholder to be fully compensated for a loss. Cover could be arranged to provide full indemnity if required, but a higher premium would result.

Deductibles are simply much larger excesses, mainly encountered in respect of commercial risks where the company compares the financial benefit of reducing premiums with the cost of bearing smaller claims itself and makes a decision to insure only in respect of larger claims.

Franchises

A franchise can involve money or time. As with an excess, an amount is specified within which all claims will be met by the insured. Should a claim fall within the franchise limit, the insurer will play no part in its settlement. Should the amount of the claim exceed the franchise limit, the insurer will settle the whole claim, including that part falling within the franchise.

Case study

Claim £450	Excess £50	Insurer pays £400	Insured pays £50
Claim £450	Franchise £500	Insurer pays £0	Insured pays £450
Claim £550	Franchise £500	Insurer pays £550	Insured pays £0

Applying this principle to time results in a deferred period after which claims will be paid. If the incident is resolved within the franchise period, there is no insurer involvement. If the incident (e.g. sickness covered by a personal accident and sickness policy) extends beyond the franchise then a claim payment would include the franchise period.

Time franchises are quite common, but money franchises are rare outside marine insurance.

Exclusions

Introduction

Any insurance contract will contain terms that indicate what is and what is not covered by the policy. The clauses which refer to what is not covered are known as exclusions, although they can also be referred to as 'exceptions'.

Specific exclusions

These relate to a particular type of insurance, or to just part of the contract.

General exclusions

These relate to the entire contract and if they come into operation usually enable the insurer to repudiate any liability under the policy.

Market exclusions

Some of the general exclusions appear in all general insurance policies:

- war and related perils;
- riot and civil commotion;
- radioactive contamination and explosive nuclear assemblies.

Others are common to all property insurance policies:

- pollution and/or contamination;
- terrorism;
- sonic bangs;
- marine policies.

All motor and liability policies will also carry a contractual liability exclusion. This exclusion enables the insurer to avoid any claims arising from a contract of which it was unaware when negotiating the contract of insurance.

Most of these exclusions are straightforward, relieving the insurer of liability for incidents that would more properly be the responsibility of the government.

The marine policies exclusion prevents the insurer becoming liable in respect of property which also forms part of a marine policy. Marine policies may similarly exclude liability for damage caused by a fire policy.

Fidelity (guarantee) insurance

Introduction

Whilst theft policies cater for the larger, more external risks, fidelity insurance policies (previously known as fidelity guarantee insurance) cover risks associated with the dishonesty of employees. This can be either small-scale pilfering or large-scale fraudulent misappropriation of funds.

Types of policy

Policies can be written in a number of ways, depending on how the insured wishes cover to be provided:

- individual policy: covers a named individual for a set amount;
- collective named policy: a schedule of named employees is produced, with either an amount of cover for each employee or a total amount (floating sum) for the policy shown;
- collective unnamed policy: this identifies employees by their roles (so the policy may show 'three accounts clerks') rather than by their names;
- blanket policy: includes all employees without showing names or positions;
- positions policy: guarantees the position for a set amount, regardless of the position-holder, who might change.

Where a floating sum insured applies, the amount will be reduced by the amount of each claim, until renewal or until an additional premium is paid to reinstate the full amount of cover.

Policy cover

The aggregate limit of indemnity, the insurer's maximum exposure in any one period of insurance, will be shown in the schedule together with the limit that applies to any one loss.

Cover is provided to people:

- employed under a contract of service or apprenticeship, or as a trainee under a government training scheme;
- whose contract of service relates to the business of the insured specified in the policy schedule;
- who are resident within the territorial limits of the policy (Great Britain) although employees temporarily working abroad would also be covered.

The policy covers the insured's property, which means money or goods, or goods that are in the insured's care and for which the insured has a legal responsibility.

The policy also specifies what constitutes fraud (essentially, an employee engaging in a dishonest act or a series of acts, or colluding with other employees in such acts) and when cover is operative (the fraudulent act(s) must occur during the period of insurance). Cover for a named individual under a policy can only be given from the date that he or she was added to the policy, even if losses occurred before that time. If a claim is made, then further losses from fraud on the part of the same individual are not covered by the policy.

It is unusual for a policy to ask the insured to identify the person responsible for the fraud, or to report the matter to the police – the decision on these matters remains the insured's. The insured must prove that any loss resulted from a fraudulent act.

Most policies allow for a period of two years after the end of the policy term, during which the fraud can be discovered and cover provided, as long as the fraud took place while the policy was current. They also include a clause that commits the current policy to covering a loss discovered outside the allowed period, as long as there is no gap in cover and both the person responsible and the loss were insured under both of the policies concerned. The lowest limit of indemnity applicable to either policy would be used as the limit of the insurer's liability for the loss.

No consequential losses resulting from the fraudulent act are covered, only the loss of the property itself. Fees for employing auditors to investigate suspected fraud can be covered if the insurer gives its written consent.

Policy extensions or endorsements

Excesses and deductibles

These are common in fidelity insurance, with any voluntary excesses applying in addition to compulsory excesses imposed. The operation of the excess is slightly different in fidelity insurance and relates to the limit set for any one loss. If a claim exceeds this limit, then only the amount of the limit will be paid, minus the amount of the excess. If a deductible applies, then the full amount of the loss minus the amount of the deductible would be paid, but still subject to the 'any one loss' limit.

Case study

Any one loss limit   £10,000

Excess   £2,000

Deductible   £2,000

Loss   £15,000

Calculation for excess: limit = 10,000   excess = 2,000   loss = 15,000
                               payment 8,000

Calculation for deductible: limit = 10,000   deductible = 2,000   loss = 15,000
                               payment = 13,000   subject to limit = 10,000.

Agency staff and consultants

These can be covered if assurances are given to the insurer that they are subject to the same working and monitoring systems and are under direct supervision.

Improper financial gain

The policy can be endorsed so that only losses arising from the responsible person having a motive of financial gain can be covered, and not losses that are committed out of malice against the insured rather than to achieve financial gain.

Inadvertent breach of method of operation

The insured would ask for the inclusion of this extension rather than risk the policy cover being invalidated because someone other than the person responsible for the loss failed to operate in an approved manner, thus, strictly speaking, resulting in failure to comply with the alteration condition in the policy.

Amendment of computer programs

This extension provides for the insurer to meet the costs of amending a program to improve security after a loss has occurred.

Fraudulent third party use of computers

Insurers will provide this cover if satisfied with the insured's access control systems and computer security policy. It applies only to fraudulent acts by non-employees.

Conditions

The general conditions are those that apply to most property insurance policies, but the condition requiring the insured to notify the insurer of any changes in the risk is very important to fidelity insurance, because of the rating of the risk being based on the working systems that the insured has in place.

Other conditions related to claims on the policy are:

- proof of claim: the insured must prove that it has suffered a loss; must also provide written notification of the claim to the insurer as soon as possible and take any reasonable steps to ensure that no further losses arise in the same way;
- subrogation rights: insurers allow themselves these in case they wish to try to recover the amount of the loss from the responsible person;
- loss deduction: any monies owing to the person responsible for the loss (salary, commission) can be used to partially offset the loss;
- recovery: the person responsible for the loss may volunteer, or be required by a court, to repay the amount of the loss and this condition sets out how it will be allocated.

Risk assessment

Proposal forms are used to assess the risk. Great emphasis is placed on the insured's procedures for obtaining references for new members of staff and upon the working, monitoring and checking systems that the insured has in place.

If individual policies are to be taken out, separate forms will have to be completed by the employer and by the person whose fidelity is to be the subject of each policy.

For blanket or unnamed policies, only the employer need complete a form, which contains details of:

- the system of supervision for employees;
- the enquiries that the insured makes before appointing new staff;
- the number of employees with responsibility for money and/or stock;
- the number of employees with no responsibility for money and/or stock.

The underwriter will be particularly interested in:

- the degree of moral hazard associated with the business, e.g. the extent to which small-scale theft is tolerated, the attitudes of the company officials;
- the extent to which stock is made up of high value items;
- trades where staff receive commission only;
- the amount of delivery work, especially where delivery is measured by a weighbridge.

If computers are central to business operations then a separate proposal and questionnaire will probably be required for the underwriter to assess this aspect of the risk.

Rating

The underwriter considers the nature of the business, the categories of employees (whether low, medium or high risk and how many in each category) and the desired any one loss and total limits of indemnity in order to decide on an appropriate rate, which is then applied to the expected wages for each class of employee or individual employee, and aggregated to give a total premium.

For blanket cover, where the whole workforce is covered, the rate will be based on the type of trade undertaken and the categories of employees, with a rate per mille (‰) being applied to expected total wages for each employee category.

Warranties

As the working systems of the insured are critical to the results of the fidelity insurance policy, the policy is likely to include warranties which aim to ensure that the insured adheres to the ways of working that have been agreed. Breach of a warranty will invalidate cover under the policy, so it is important for the insured to follow any warranty requirements very closely.

Examples of warranties would be those requiring references for all employees, and relating to auditing systems, cash handling systems and the security aspects of computer use.

Fire and special perils insurance

Introduction

Cover for what is known as 'material damage' can be provided by the standard ABI fire and special perils policy wording agreed with insurers, by an 'all risks' policy, or by a Lloyd's fire policy.

Standard fire and special perils policy

The ABI wordings are available to help members, but are not compulsory. In practice, the wordings are generally followed.

Because of the importance of this class of cover, the policy wording is reproduced below, with explanations of the cover where necessary. Any exclusions are also shown.

Wording	Commentary
The insurer agrees (subject to the terms, definition, exclusions, provisions and conditions of this policy)	Indemnity will be provided by the policy only if the requirements of all of the parts of the policy are observed.
that if after payment of the first premium any of the property insured described in the schedule be lost destroyed or damaged by any of the perils specified in the schedule during the period of insurance (or any subsequent period for which the insurer accepts a renewal premium)	The schedule must identify clearly the risk to be insured. Property would be buildings, contents, stock and other items.
	Most policies are written on an annual basis.

Wording

the insurer will pay to the insured the value of the property at the time of the loss or destruction or the amount of the damage or at the insurer's option reinstate or replace such property or any part of it

provided that the liability of the insurer under the policy shall not exceed

(i) in the whole the total sum insured or in respect of any item its sum insured at the time of the loss destruction or damage

(ii) the sum insured remaining after deduction for any other loss destruction or damage occurring during the same period of insurance, unless the insurer shall have agreed to reinstate any such sum insured

This policy incorporates the schedule, specification and endorsements which shall be read together as one contract. Words and expressions to which specific meaning is given in any part of this policy shall have the same meaning wherever they appear.

Commentary

The insurer's maximum liability under the policy is the total sum insured.

If a claim is made, then the total sum insured is reduced by the amount of the claim for the remainder of the period of insurance, unless it is reinstated by payment of an additional premium.

Wording

Definition

The word DAMAGE in capital letters shall mean loss or destruction of or damage to the property insured.

Commentary

This saves the full phrase having to be used each time.

Perils	Exclusions	Commentary
A FIRE	DAMAGE caused by: (a) explosion resulting from fire (b) earthquake or subterranean fire (c) (i) its own spontaneous fermentation or heating or (c) (ii) its undergoing any heating process or any process involving the application of heat	For fire cover to apply, there must be actual ignition of the property, smouldering is not covered, the thing which is on fire should not be intended to be on fire and the fire must be accidental or fortuitous in origin in so far as the insured in concerned.
LIGHTNING EXPLOSION (i) of boilers (ii) of gas	DAMAGE caused by earthquake or subterranean fire	Any damage whose proximate cause is fire will be covered (see separate section on PROXIMATE CAUSE). If fire from spontaneous fermentation occurs,

Perils	Exclusions	Commentary
used for domestic purposes only		then only the damage to the item which caught fire spontaneously is excluded. Domestic means any purpose which would ordinarily be found in a home.
B EXPLOSION	DAMAGE (a) caused by or consisting of the bursting of a boiler economiser or other vessel machine or apparatus in which internal pressure is due to steam only and belonging to or under the control of the insured	Damage caused by the explosion of a steam pressure vessel which neither belongs to nor is under the control of the insured, is covered even if on the insured's premises.
	(b) in respect of and originating in any vessel machinery or apparatus, or its contents, belonging to or under the control of the insured which requires to be examined to comply with any statutory regulations unless such vessel	The explosion peril provides cover for the perils otherwise excluded under the standard fire peril: concussion damage by explosion of vessels used for other than domestic purposes.

Perils	Exclusions	Commentary
	machinery or apparatus shall be the subject of a policy or other contract providing the required inspection service	
	(c) by fire resulting from explosion	
	(d) by explosion	
	(i) of boilers	
	(ii) of gas	
	used for domestic purposes only	
	(e) by pressure waves caused by aircraft or other aerial devices travelling at sonic or supersonic speeds	
C AIRCRAFT or other aerial devices or articles dropped therefrom	DAMAGE (a) by pressure waves caused by aircraft or other aerial devices travelling at sonic or supersonic speeds (b) by fire	This relates to damage caused other than by fire.
D RIOT CIVIL COMMOTION STRIKERS LOCKED OUT WORKERS or persons taking	DAMAGE (a) arising from confiscation requisition or destruction by order	Following the Public Order Act 1986, the definition of riot is that 12 or more people must be participating in the

Perils	Exclusions	Commentary
part in labour disturbances or malicious persons acting on behalf of or in connection with any political organisation	of the government or any public authority (b) arising from cessation of work (c) by fire caused by strikers locked-out workers or persons taking part in labour disturbances or malicious persons	use or threat of unlawful violence for a common purpose. The offence of violent disorder requires three people to be using or threatening unlawful violence, but they do not need to be operating with a common purpose.
E RIOT CIVIL COMMOTION STRIKERS LOCKED-OUT WORKERS or persons taking part in labour disturbances or MALICIOUS PERSONS	(a) DAMAGE arising from confiscation requisition or destruction by order of the government or any public authority (b) DAMAGE arising from cessation of work (c) DAMAGE by fire caused by strikers locked-out workers or persons taking part in labour disturbances or malicious persons (d) as regards DAMAGE (other than by fire or explosion) directly caused by malicious	This provides cover for malicious damage, caused by persons acting without a political motive. Any damage intentionally caused to property is regarded as malicious damage.

Perils	Exclusions	Commentary
	persons not acting on behalf of or in connection with any political organisation	
	(i) DAMAGE by theft	
	(ii) DAMAGE in respect of any building which is empty or not in use	
	(iii) the first £ of each and every loss as ascertained after the application of any condition of average (underinsurance)	
F RIOT OR CIVIL COMMOTION in respect of DAMAGE caused by fire only	DAMAGE arising from (a) confiscation requisition or destruction by order of the government or any public authority (b) cessation of work	A lower premium rate applies if only this restricted cover is required.
G EARTHQUAKE		As damage from this risk is rare in Great Britain it is widely available.

Perils	**Exclusions**	**Commentary**
H EARTHQUAKE in respect of DAMAGE caused by fire only		
J EARTHQUAKE	DAMAGE caused by fire	
K SUBTERRANEAN FIRE		The underwriter will be put on enquiry by the insured specifically requesting this cover and will undertake investigations into the risk before granting specific cover.
L Fire only resulting from the property's own SPONTANEOUS FERMENTATION OR HEATING		The underwriter will be put on enquiry by the insured specifically requesting this cover and will undertake investigations into the risk before granting specific cover.
M STORM	(a) DAMAGE by (i) the escape of water from	

Perils	Exclusions	Commentary
	the normal confines of any natural or artificial water course lake reservoir canal or dam	
	(ii) inundation from the sea	
	(b) DAMAGE attributable solely to change in the water table level	
	(c) DAMAGE by lightning frost subsidence ground heave or landslip	
	(d) Damage in respect of moveable property in the open, fences and gates	
	(e) the first £ of each and every loss in respect of each separate premises as ascertained after the application of any condition of average (underinsurance)	
N STORM OR FLOOD	(a) DAMAGE attributable solely to change in the water table level	The calculation of average requires a reduction in the amount of a claim payment if the sum

Perils	Exclusions	Commentary
	(b) DAMAGE by lightning frost subsidence ground heave or landslip	insured proves to have been less than the true value at risk in the event of a claim. (See separate section on AVERAGE.)
	(c) Damage in respect of moveable property in the open, fences and gates	
	(d) the first £ of each and every loss in respect of each separate premises as ascertained after the application of any condition of average (underinsurance)	
P ESCAPE OF WATER FROM ANY TANK APPARATUS OR PIPE	(a) DAMAGE by water discharged or leaking from any automatic sprinkler installation	
	(b) DAMAGE in respect of any building which is empty or not in use	
	(c) the first £ of each and every loss in respect of each separate premises as ascertained after the application of any condition of average (underinsurance)	

Perils	Exclusions	Commentary
Q IMPACT by any road vehicle or animal not belonging to or under the control of the insured or any occupier of the premises or their respective employees		
R IMPACT by any road vehicle or animal	in respect of road vehicles or animals belonging to or under the control of the insured or any occupier of the premises or their respective employees the first £ of each and every loss as ascertained after the application of any condition of average (underinsurance)	
S ACCIDENTAL ESCAPE OF WATER FROM ANY AUTOMATIC SPRINKLER INSTALLATION in the premises not caused by (a) freezing while the		

Perils	Exclusions	Commentary
building in so far as it is in the insured's ownership or tenancy is empty or not in use		
(b) explosion earthquake subterranean fire or heat caused by fire		
T SUBSIDENCE or GROUND HEAVE of any part of the site on which the property stands or LANDSLIP	(a) DAMAGE to yards, car parks, roads, pavements, walls, gates and fences unless also affecting a building insured hereby	Subsidence can be caused by the uneven settlement of made-up ground, underground workings such as mines, building on mixed soil types or the removal of moisture from clay soil often by tree roots in very dry conditions.
	(b) DAMAGE caused by or consisting of	
	(i) the normal settlement or bedding down of new structures	Heave has the opposite effect, lifting the ground when the moisture in the soil increases.
	(ii) the settlement or movement of made-up ground	Landslip is a small landslide.
	(iii) coastal or river erosion	
	(iv) defective design or workmanship	

Perils	**Exclusions**	**Commentary**
	or the use of defective materials	
	(v) fire subterranean fire explosion earthquake or the escape of water from any tank apparatus or pipe	
	(c) DAMAGE which originated prior to the inception of the cover	
	(d) DAMAGE resulting from	
	(i) demolition construction structural alteration or repair of any property or	
	(ii) groundworks or excavation	
	at the same premises	
	(e) the first £ of each and every loss at each separate premises as ascertained after the application of any condition of average (underinsurance)	

Special condition

In so far as this insurance relates to damage caused by subsidence ground heave or landslip

(a) the insured shall notify the insurer immediately they become aware of any demolition, groundworks, excavation or construction being carried out on any adjoining site;

(b) the insurer shall then have the right to vary the terms or cancel this cover

General exclusions

The general exclusions that apply to the fire and special perils policy are:

- war risks;
- ionising radiation or contamination by radioactivity;
- terrorism in Northern Ireland (there is limited cover for terrorism in the rest of Great Britain under the Special Provision – Terrorism. See separate section on TERRORISM COVER);
- pollution or contamination;
- risks covered by marine policies.

General provisions

The pro rata condition of average applies to the policy.

The other provision relates to the interest that a purchaser of a property may have in the property if it is damaged between exchange of contracts and completion. The provision allows for the purchaser to be compensated for the loss instead of the insured selling the property, but only to the extent of the insured's interest in the property.

General conditions

These are common to most commercial policies:

- voidable policy: the policy is voidable at the option of the insurers in the event of there being any misrepresentation or non-disclosure of a material fact;
- alteration: if the insured fails to notify the insurer of an alteration to the risk then that part of the policy affected by the non-disclosure is automatically avoided;

- warranties: breach of a warranty permits the insurer to avoid the policy if there has been an increase in risk as a result. The insurer has the option to avoid the policy from the date of the breach.

Checklist: Claims conditions

These are common to most commercial policies:

- action by the insured: sets out the things that an insured must do in the event of a claim;
- fraud: any fraud invalidates the policy cover;
- reinstatement: gives the insurer the right to reinstate the property rather than to pay monetary compensation, which it may wish to do if it can obtain a replacement at a wholesale value, or if the insured refuses to change a claim amount that the insurer regards as excessive and more than the costs of reinstating the property;
- rights of entry: the insurer is given the right to enter or take possession of the property after a claim and to take possession of and deal with goods or property in a reasonable manner to reduce their outlay;
- contribution and average (see separate sections);
- subrogation (see separate section);
- arbitration: action to be taken to resolve disputes between insured and insurer about the amount payable under the policy, not about the insurer's liability under the policy.

Reinstatement Memorandum

Insurers agree to provide cover for property under a material damage policy on the basis of its value as new, rather than deducting an amount for wear and tear from any claim settlement or expecting the insured to contribute an amount for betterment if property is replaced as new.

Policies written subject to the Reinstatement Memorandum allow for the value of property to be calculated on the cost of its rebuilding, replacement, repair or restoration to a condition equivalent to that it enjoyed when new.

If the property is only partially destroyed the insurer's maximum liability is the estimated cost of reinstatement if it had been wholly destroyed.

Average applies if 85% of the cost of reinstating the whole of the property exceeds its sum insured when damaged. This is different from the usual way in which average applies, which is to compare the value of the property at the time of loss with the sum insured.

If average applies, the insurer's liability is determined by:

$$\frac{\text{sum insured} \times \text{loss}}{\text{reinstatement cost of whole property at time of reinstatement}}$$

Special conditions apply to the Reinstatement Memorandum:

- the insurer's liability is limited to the proportion that the declared value bears to the cost of reinstatement;
- the insurer's liability for partial loss is limited by the amount payable in the event of a total loss;
- the day one cover applies only if reinstatement begins and progresses without delay, payment is only due once reinstatement costs have been incurred by the insured and if no other insurance exists that is on a different basis of reinstatement.

Inflation

The effects of inflation can result in a sum insured proving inadequate if the policy includes the option for the property to be reinstated. The most common means of negating the impact of inflation are to include the Escalator (Appreciation in Value) clause in the policy or to write the policy on a day one basis.

Escalator clause

This provides for automatic increases in the sum insured, at a rate chosen by the insured, each day during the period of insurance. In return for this, the insured pays an additional 50% of the figure produced by applying the figure chosen to the first year's premium. So, if the premium is £100 and the insured chooses 10% as the figure for inflation, 50% of £10 gives an additional premium of £5.

The escalator clause applies to buildings and contents, but not to stock; no return of premium is given if inflation is less than expected, and the revised sum insured and percentage rate for the next period must be supplied at renewal.

Day one basis

This type of cover aims to combine the best features of other inflation-combating schemes.

A wording identical to the Reinstatement Memorandum is incorporated in the policy, with the insured being required to provide a declared value for the property to be insured. This declared value is the reinstatement cost of the property at the inception of the policy – hence 'day one' cover. The premium is calculated on the basis of this value. Fees and debris removal costs are included in the value assessment to the extent that they are covered in the rest of the policy.

Special conditions apply to the day one basis, as to the Reinstatement Memorandum:

- the declared value must be notified at policy inception or renewal as otherwise the insured may be underinsured;
- the insurer's liability is limited to the proportion that the declared value bears to the cost of reinstatement;
- the insurer's liability for partial loss is limited by the amount payable in the event of a total loss;
- the day one cover applies only if reinstatement begins and progresses without delay, payment is only due once reinstatement costs have been incurred by the insured and if no other insurance exists that is on a different basis of reinstatement;
- if reinstatement is not carried out average will apply in the normal way;
- additional machinery acquired during the period of insurance, or alterations/additions to buildings, is covered if not subject to other insurances. The additional premium for this would be included when the premium was adjusted at the end of the policy term.

Floating or blanket covers

If insurance is to be arranged for more than one set of premises, then it can be written on a floating basis to cover stock, contents or buildings under a single sum insured for each type of property, regardless of the number of premises.

Declarations of stock values held in each location must be provided by the insured and the premium is based on the appropriate average for the values declared.

All risks cover

Many parts of the all risks wording are the same as the standard fire and special perils policy, but rather than identifying those perils that are covered under the policy and those excluded, the all risks policy covers any risk that is not specifically excluded.

The wording of the policy cover granted is very similar to the fire and special perils policy, but the definition of damage includes 'accidental':

The insurer agrees (subject to the terms, definition, exclusions, provisions and conditions of this policy) that if after payment of the first premium any of the property insured described in the schedule be accidentally lost destroyed or damaged during the period of insurance (or any subsequent period for which the insurer accepts a renewal premium) the insurer will pay to the insured the value of the property at the time of its loss or destruction or the amount of the damage or at the insurer's option reinstate or replace such property or any part of it provided that the liability of the insurer under the policy shall not exceed

(i) in the whole the total sum insured or in respect of any item its sum insured or any other limit of liability stated in the schedule at the time of the loss destruction or damage

(ii) the sum insured (or limit) remaining after deduction for any other loss destruction or damage occurring during the same period of insurance, unless the insurer shall have agreed to reinstate any such sum insured (or limit).

This policy incorporates the schedule, specification and endorsements which shall be read together as one contract. Words and expressions to which specific meaning is given in any part of this policy shall have the same meaning wherever they appear.

Definition

The word DAMAGE in capital letters shall mean accidental loss or destruction of or damage to the property insured.

The policy covers fire and the special perils numbered A to S in the fire and special perils wording reproduced on pages 87–100 above, plus accidental damage. It incorporates limits of liability which can be imposed by the insurer or incorporated at the insured's request.

Checklist: Policy exclusions, all risks

The all risks policy excludes damage arising from or to:

*   inherent defect, defective workmanship, explosion of boilers, pressure waves from aircraft;
*   rot or vermin damage, deterioration, theft or attempted theft, leakage of joints in boilers, mechanical or electrical breakdown;
*   pollution or contamination other than from a defined peril;

- subsidence, fraud or disappearance of property;
- a building's own collapse;
- moveable property in the open, fences and gates from adverse weather;
- fire from heating or production processes;
- freezing, escape of water or malicious damage to unoccupied buildings;
- valuables, goods in transit, glass, computers, money and non-negotiable instruments;
- road vehicles, buildings being constructed and materials, land, livestock and crops;
- marine policies;
- more specific insurances;
- war;
- radioactive contamination;
- terrorism in Northern Ireland.

The policy is subject to a deductible, which the insured can choose to increase.

The all risks and the fire and special perils policy can be extended to include cover for professional fees incurred following a loss, debris removal and loss of rent while damaged buildings are unoccupiable.

Warranties and clauses

Clauses can be added to material damage policies to extend the cover available, or as warranties which can be incorporated to require the insured to do or not to do something.

All policies contain one warranty which relates to the need to ensure that industrial waste is cleared at the end of each day or at relevant intervals. An example of such a warranty applied to the power woodworking trade is: 'All sawdust, shavings and other trade refuse to be swept up and bagged at the end of each working day and removed from the premises at least once a week.'

The ABI produces recommended wordings for some of the more common clauses.

Clauses affect cover in the following ways:

- contract price clause: covers the element of profit that would have been made by the seller on goods which were sold before the loss but damaged before delivery to the buyer;
- mortgagees, freeholders and lessors clause: covers the insured for any change in the risk or act or omission by such people which increases the risk without the insured's knowledge;
- non-invalidation clause: cover is not affected by any breach of a

condition for which the insured is not responsible;

- subrogation waiver clause: if cover is granted to a company in a large group, the insurers agree not to pursue any subrogation rights that may arise against another company in the same group;
- temporary removal, temporary removal (documents), temporary removal (computer records) clauses: covers goods (or documents or computer records) which have to be moved from the premises on a temporary basis. This has to be for the purpose of cleaning or repair for goods, but the purpose of the removal is not specified for the other items;
- electrical clause: plant is only covered for electrical breakdown if the fire caused spreads to other items of plant as well;
- motor vehicles: cover is provided for motor vehicles only if the amount provided by any more specific policy has been exceeded;
- metalworkers' extension: cover can be provided for property on certain premises other than those insured;
- workman's clause: minor alterations in the risk, or changes due to maintenance or repairs, can be made without invalidating the cover;
- notice clause: insurers must be notified of any changes concerning unoccupied buildings.

Lloyd's fire policy

This is shorter than the ABI standard policy. It covers:

- fire;
- lightning;
- fire resulting from explosion;
- explosion resulting from fire on the insured premises;
- explosion of domestic boilers or of gas used for domestic purposes or for lighting or heating.

It excludes:

- damage to dynamos, transformers, motors, wiring, mains or other electrical appliances caused by short-circuiting, over-running, excessive pressure or leakage by electricity;
- ionising radiation or radioactive contamination;
- war, riot and civil commotion;
- damage to computer records;
- terrorism damage in Northern Ireland.

Other perils

Policies for the perils below can also be arranged in the fire insurance market:

- hail damage to crops and greenhouses;
- accidental damage to underground and overhead services;
- leakage of oil or other liquids;
- theft damage to buildings;
- escape of molten metal.

Checklist: Risk assessment, fire and special perils

The responsibility for assessing a risk will usually rest on a risk surveyor employed by the insurer to gather all of the necessary information and present this to the underwriter in report form.

Information will be provided on:

- space heating;
- process heating;
- flammable liquids;
- reactive chemicals;
- grinding processes or reduction to fine particles;
- construction;
- housekeeping;
- combustible packing materials;
- undivided areas;
- high piled storage;
- damageable contents;
- multiple occupancy.

Any factors likely to improve the risk would also be included within the report:

- fire resistant construction;
- automatic fire alarms;
- hose reels and extinguishers;
- sprinklers.

Rating

Most insurers use a rating table of normal risks in each trade. There is a classification system for trades attracting different levels of risk, so that a stone-built church would represent a very low level of risk, while a dry cleaning operation would represent quite a high level of risk.

Once the basic rate has been found for a normal risk in the appropriate class of risk, the premium will be loaded for any adverse features, which would make the risk more likely to happen or more likely to have a severe effect if it did happen, or to make it more difficult to deal with the effects of the peril. A discount can then be given for any good features, which reduce the likely incidence or severity of the risk.

Glass insurance

Introduction

Replacing broken glass can be expensive for a business and it is important to arrange adequate cover. Glass insurance is increasingly only available as an addition to another material damage policy and difficult to find as a stand-alone policy, with many insurers writing the business only to accommodate known clients.

Cover

Cover for 'all risks' is provided for destruction or damage to fixed glass, which includes:

- windows;
- door glazing;
- fanlights;
- showcases;
- fixed mirror glass;
- glazed partitions;
- and, if desired, can be limited to external glass only.

Extensions

Reimbursement of costs for any boarding-up necessary is provided as an extension to the policy, which can also be extended to include:

- damage to shopfront contents from broken glazing;
- washbasins and sanitary fittings in hairdressing salons and hotels.

Exclusions

Cover excludes scratching or chipping and any damage to letterwork or ornamentation unless this results from the breakage of the glass.

As damage caused by fire, lightning and explosion would be covered by a more specific fire/material damage policy, it is standard practice for a glass policy to exclude these perils.

A £50 excess is common.

Rating

Premium will most likely be based on a fixed rate per cent applied to the value of the glass to be covered.

Underwriting considerations

In deciding whether to accept a risk, and the rate and terms that should apply, an underwriter will look at:

Previous loss history: especially if there have been regular claims. The option open to the underwriter would be to decline the risk; or, if it seems that the proposer has taken action to minimise or eliminate losses, to increase either the rate, or the excess, or both.

Location: if the property is in an area subject to vandalism, e.g. close to a football ground, then the underwriter would probably decline the risk, or impose a high excess to accommodate a known insured.

Occupation: whether or not a building is occupied, and if so, for what it is used, is an important consideration. Unoccupied buildings are prone to malicious damage and vandalism and insurers therefore tend to decline cover for them. Buildings used as bookmakers, social clubs and public houses, amongst others, represent an increased hazard, for which the underwriter would impose an increased excess and possibly insist on the use of protective grilles.

Construction: gives a good indication of possible risk. Greenhouses are of lightweight structure and therefore present a greater risk: cover would usually be declined other than for a catastrophe risk, when a very large excess (e.g. £500) would probably be imposed. Damage to offices built largely of glass (what is known as 'curtain glazing') can be very expensive, costing up to £2,000 to replace one panel, so a high excess (e.g. £250) would probably be imposed.

Unusual glass: such as stained glass in churches, or other coloured glass, costs more than normal to replace and warrants the rate being increased by 50% or more, depending on the location of the building.

Claims

If the quality of the fixings is improved following replacement of broken glass, an amount for betterment will be deducted from the claim.

Goods in transit (inland transit) insurance

Introduction

Also known as 'inland transit' insurance, this provides cover for 'all risks' predominantly fire, accidental damage and theft risks for goods being transported.

In the event of a loss, the insurer has the option under the policy to repair or replace the goods or to make a cash payment in settlement of the claim.

Policy cover

The goods are covered during loading at the insured's premises, during the journey to the consignee, and during unloading and delivery to the consignee, including an overnight stay if this is necessary and the insurer accepts the security arrangements that have been put in place.

The normal territorial limits apply; outside the UK goods would more properly be covered under a marine or aviation policy.

Cover can be limited to fire, collision and overturning only, if the insurer is concerned at the security protection for the goods, or if the insured is very confident in the security protection in place.

Warranties may be imposed on the policy to reinforce the need for care in respect of the theft cover and may require the insured to put in place specific security measures and to ensure that these are followed at all times.

Means of transport

Road, rail and post are covered by the policy. Delivery of goods by road may be done using road hauliers, probably operating under conditions of carriage which limit their liability to a set amount per tonne (and a lesser amount per tonne for partial losses). Members of the Road Haulage Association apply standard approved conditions to all contracts.

Warning

It is important to check the conditions of carriage used by a carrier to determine those losses that will be covered, those that will be excluded and the limits that will apply.

Policy limits

The policy can be written either on a specified vehicle basis, with cover restricted to agreed limits for each transit in a specified vehicle, or on a declaration basis, where the policy is rated on the estimated annual turnover of deliveries and is then adjusted at the end of the year following a declaration from the insured of the actual figures. The specified vehicle basis is more appropriate for smaller traders and the declaration policy for larger operations.

The declaration policy has two limits: any one loss and any one consignment. A loss could represent a number of consignments, with each consignment being one delivery to one customer at one address, using the same consignment note.

It is essential to choose limits that accurately reflect the likely sums involved. The any one loss limit may need to cover more than one full load if vehicles travel in convoy or are parked together overnight, because of the accumulation risk.

Exclusions

The policy excludes:

- wear and tear;
- consequential loss;
- confiscation by customs or government agencies;
- property insured under a more specific policy;
- goods put in storage during transit;
- losses from weather conditions on open trailers unless the goods are suitably protected from the elements;
- the loading and unloading risks associated with fragile goods;
- deterioration of refrigerated stock unless arising from theft or accident covered by the policy;
- the first amount of any claim, by imposing a small excess.

Extensions

Policy cover can be extended to include:

- ropes and tarpaulins stolen from open trailers;
- costs involved in removing or reloading or dismantling goods following an accident;
- limited cover for sea transits.

Checklist: Risk assessment

The underwriter will assess the risk on the basis of the:

- occupation of the insured;
- goods being carried;
- packaging of the goods;
- insured's location;
- vehicles being used;
- security of the vehicles;
- overnight risk;
- conditions of carriage;
- limit – any one loss or any one consignment;
- previous loss history.

Rating

For the specified vehicle policy, the premium rate is based upon the limits set for each vehicle and a rate per cent will be applied to these.

For the declaration policy, a rate per cent or per mille will apply to the annual carryings of the company. This figure will be estimated and adjusted at the end of the policy term following the declaration made by the insured of the actual figures which represent the goods carried. Insurers may have a scale of rates for specified occupations, or adjust a base rate individually in the light of their assessment of the risk.

Hazard

Introduction

When an underwriter considers a risk, he or she will be interested in a number of features, two of which are the frequency with which risks of the type being proposed actually suffer losses and, when such losses do occur, their likely severity.

There is a correlation between frequency and severity – the greater the frequency, the lower the severity is the usual pattern. This becomes clear if we consider road traffic accidents and aviation accidents. The former represent a high-frequency, low-severity type of risk, the latter is an example of the opposite profile; a low-frequency, high-severity risk.

Hazard is a term given to any factor that would influence either the frequency or severity of a peril (the event giving rise to a loss, e.g. fire) if it occurred. In relation to a fire policy, hazard could be that the subject-matter of insurance forms part of a company using chemicals in a manufacturing process, or it could be a proposer with a history of arson attacks on his property.

You will note that these two examples of hazard relate to different things: one represents a physical aspect of the risk (chemicals) and one relates more to the possible behaviour of the proposer (arson attacks).

Physical hazard

This is the hazard that relates to the physical characteristics of the subject-matter of insurance (property, or some event that leads to a liability being created, or to the loss of a legal right).

Examples of physical hazard are:

- the construction of buildings, fire resistance, security features (property);
- hazardous substances in the workplace, heavy or unguarded machinery (employer's liability);
- modification of a car to increase performance, high mileage, use in central London (motor);

117

- an existing medical condition or a dangerous hobby such as deep sea diving (life).

Moral hazard

The attitude of the proposer (or insured) to the risk is referred to as moral hazard. This is difficult to assess but could make the difference between a good risk and a poor risk. If an insured owns an expensive car, treasures it and drives it carefully so as not to harm it, the risk will be that much better than the same car driven by someone who cares nothing for it and drives recklessly.

Examples of moral hazard are:

- the insured being careless about the safety of others;
- making fraudulent or exaggerated claims;
- dishonesty in relation to previous insurances.

In the example given originally, of a history of arson attacks on property owned by the insured, this may reveal fraudulent behaviour on the part of the insured, or indicate problems in the relationships that the insured has with others. It could also be entirely innocent and coincidental.

The underwriter must exercise judgement in determining the extent of the impact of either physical or moral hazard on the risk proposed.

Household contents insurance

Introduction

Household contents are personal effects and goods that belong to the insured or a member of his or her family who is also living in the property. Structures are not covered, as these would be the subject of BUILDINGS INSURANCE.

Policy cover

The basic contents policy covers the following perils:

- fire, lightning, explosion and earthquake and smoke;
- theft or attempted theft;
- riot, civil commotion, strikes, labour or political disturbances;
- malicious damage or vandalism;
- storm or flood;
- subsidence, ground heave or landslip;
- collision involving aircraft or aerial devices or articles dropped from them, vehicles or animals;
- falling trees or branches;
- breakage or collapse of television or radio receiving aerials; aerial fittings or masts;
- water or oil escaping from any fixed water or heating installation or domestic appliance.

The policy can also be extended, either automatically or non-automatically, to include:

- accidental breakage of fixed glass, mirrors, plate glass and ceramic hobs;
- loss or damage to contents in the open within the boundaries of the property;
- loss or damage to contents elsewhere in the British Isles;
- alternative accommodation if made necessary by one of the perils covered by the policy;

- accidental damage to televisions, videos, audio and computer equipment;
- accidental loss or damage to contents while in transit between homes by professional removal contractors;
- replacement costs for new locks or mechanisms following theft of keys;
- preparation of new title deeds;
- loss or damage to freezer contents.

All policies now cover the insured's potential liabilities for defects in buildings previously owned or occupied by the insured and potential liabilities as a private individual and as an employer of domestic servants, incurred in respect of buildings occupied by the insured, including temporary holiday residences. It applies to accidental injury to people or accidental damage to property, anywhere in the UK, and is usually subject to a limit of indemnity of £1 million.

Checklist: Optional extensions

In addition to the basic policy, for a higher premium, cover can be provided for:

- 'all risks' cover for property whilst away from the insured address, both specified and unspecified items;
- money and credit cards;
- bicycles;
- caravans;
- small craft;
- sports equipment;
- personal accident benefits;
- hospital cash benefits;
- creditor insurance;
- domestic animals;
- legal expenses.

Exclusions

Limits of indemnity, excesses and exclusions vary depending on which sections of the policy are being called upon.

The most significant are:

- for theft of cash, currency, money or stamps, forcible or violent entry to the building may be necessary before cover applies;
- accidental damage excludes damage while the building is let, or from

wear and tear, wet or dry rot, fungus, vermin or insects, and would not cover clothing, contact lenses, stamps, money, coins, medals, plants, food or drink;

- for works of art, stamp collections, jewellery, precious metals or furs, a single article limit of not more than 5% of the total sum insured will apply and the total value of valuables will be limited to not more than one-third of the sum insured.

Individual sections will impose their own specific exclusions.

Indemnity

Introduction

The principle of indemnity is central to insurance. Essentially it means that following a loss, the insured should be returned to the exact same financial position as he or she was in before the loss occurred.

However, the interpretation of what constitutes indemnity is slightly more difficult.

Insurable interest

As it is the insured's financial interest in the subject-matter of insurance that is insured, it is not possible for the insured to receive more than the amount of that interest in the event of a claim.

Both of these concepts depend on it being possible to allocate a financial value to the subject-matter of insurance. This is true for most general insurance policies, but not so for policies such as life assurance where the subject-matter of insurance is someone's life and it would be almost impossible to place a monetary value on that life.

Life and personal accident policies are not therefore policies of indemnity, but instead guarantee to pay a fixed prearranged sum on the happening of the insured event. Nevertheless, the underwriter of such a policy would take care to ensure that the amounts of cover being sought under the policies were not excessive when compared to the amount of insurable interest.

How to indemnify?

In the event of a claim, the insurer has a number of options as to how to provide indemnity to the insured. These are:

- a monetary payment;
- repair;
- replacement;
- reinstatement.

Payment to the insured

This is by far the most common method of providing indemnity, with a cheque being sent to the insured once a figure for settlement of the claim has been agreed. It is always the means by which claims are settled in liability insurance. If settlement must also be made with third parties, payment will be made to them direct, rather than via the insured.

Repair

Common in motor insurance particularly, where insurers pay for repairs to be made to vehicles damaged in road traffic accidents. This gives them the opportunity to negotiate prices direct with the garage, or to authorise garages where repairs can be carried out, giving them much greater control on prices and the quality of repairs. The insured signs a document to confirm his or her satisfaction with the repairs before the car is released. This method is convenient also for insureds, as it saves them having to pay for repairs themselves and then be out of pocket while they claim from their insurer.

Replacement

Most common in glass insurance, where insurers can negotiate discounts with glaziers because of the large amounts of business placed with them. The use by motor insurers of companies such as Autoglass is another example of replacement – the insured rings a number provided with the policy in the event of the windscreen breaking and Autoglass goes to a location convenient to the insured and fits a replacement screen. The insured's problem is resolved quickly and conveniently, the insurer can negotiate discounts and also can cut down on fraudulent claims where small motoring bills are passed off as claims for replacement windscreens by unscrupulous garages and insureds.

Reinstatement

This is a very specialised method of providing indemnity, used in property insurance. It involves the insurer electing to return an insured property to its pre-loss condition, rather than to compensate the insured for the loss. Once the decision to reinstate has been made, the insurer must bear whatever costs are necessary to achieve the work, even if these exceed the sum insured under the policy. This method of providing indemnity is almost never used now.

The Fires (Prevention) Metropolis Act 1774 imposes a duty on insurers to ensure that any monies paid to the insured in respect of fire damage are spent on reinstating the building, if anyone with an interest in the property is suspicious that fraud has been involved in the claim or that the building has deliberately been set on fire.

The measurement of indemnity

This depends on the type of insurance.

Property

The way to determine indemnity in respect of the loss of property is not to consider the cost of the property, but to look at its value at the date of loss and at the place of the loss.

If there has been an increase in value then the insured is entitled to that increased amount as indemnity, but equally, if the value has diminished, then the insured is only entitled to that lesser amount. No allowance is made for sentimental value or for loss of profits.

Buildings

Indemnity for buildings is essentially the cost of repair or reconstruction at the time of loss, less an amount for what is known as 'betterment' (where a building is better after having been repaired than it was before the loss, e.g. new wiring having been installed as part of repairs).

As the market value of buildings may be less than the cost of replacing or repairing a building, other measures of indemnity are also used for buildings:

- the cost of repair or reinstatement less an allowance for depreciation, if the insured intends to repair or reinstate the property;
- reinstatement costs minus depreciation, if the insurer believes that the insured does not intend to reinstate the property, but cannot prove it;
- reinstatement costs, if the insurer feels that only the market value of a building should be provided as indemnity, but cannot prove that there is a market for that type of property and cannot show what the market value would have been;
- market value of the building minus the value of the site, if the insured was in the process of selling the property at the time of loss.

Machinery and contents (but not stock)

Indemnity is the cost of repair or replacement, less an allowance for depreciation. If there is a second-hand market for the property, a second-hand replacement plus costs is indemnity.

Stock in trade

For manufacturers, indemnity is the cost of replacing the goods destroyed to the condition they were in before the loss. For raw materials, this is replacement plus delivery costs, for other stock, these costs plus labour and other production costs to match state of production of goods lost.

For retailers, indemnity is the cost of replacing the stock lost and of any transport and handling costs.

A reduction may be made for obsolescence if the replacement costs are higher than the value of the lost goods is likely to be once remade.

Case study

As an example of this, think of a product that has been very popular, but only for a short lifetime. If the manufacturer lost stock at a time when the value of the products was high, but the value of the product dropped before stock could be replaced, then to pay the full pre-loss value without taking account of obsolescence would be to provide the insured with more than indemnity.

Pecuniary insurances

In policies such as fidelity guarantee, indemnity will be the amount needed to compensate the insured for any losses through the dishonesty of its employees.

For business interruption policies, the difference between the profit likely to have been made if the loss had not occurred, and that actually made, forms the basis of indemnity.

Liability insurance

Indemnity is the amount of any court award made against the insured, or negotiated out-of-court settlement, plus associated costs and expenses.

Salvage

If an insurer compensates the insured for the full value of lost or damaged property, then any residual value in the property belongs to the insurer, as otherwise the insured would have received more than indemnity.

Suppose that a car is stolen and not recovered. The insurer pays the insured the full market value of the car. Three weeks later the vehicle is recovered, in a damaged condition. As the insured has already been indemnified, the car is now the property of the insurer, which may take whatever steps it thinks fit to recover some of its costs. The vehicle will be sold as salvage and the insurer will have recouped some of its outlay.

VAT

If the insured is able to reclaim VAT from the Customs and Excise, then indemnity will be the replacement cost of the property, less VAT. If the insured is not able to reclaim VAT, indemnity will be the full replacement value including the VAT component.

Limited indemnity

In some cases, the insured will receive less than indemnity in the event of a claim.

Excess

If an EXCESS, DEDUCTIBLE or FRANCHISE applies to the policy, the insured will have to bear this part of any claim and will not have the amount reimbursed by the insurer.

Sum insured

If a policy has a sum insured specified then indemnity cannot exceed the sum insured, even if the insured's loss is greater. Equally, for policies such as liability insurance which specify a limit of liability, indemnity is that limit (though additional costs may be paid).

Average

If a claim occurs and the insured is found to have not insured the full value of the property, then the insurer's liability will be reduced in the same proportion as the underinsurance if the policy carries an AVERAGE clause. Average applies mostly to commercial insurances, although it has been introduced to some extent on household buildings insurance.

Warning

It is important to review sums insured regularly, especially in times of significant inflation, to ensure that they remain in line with potential losses and that they represent the full value of the property.

Policy limits

If the policy specifies a limit, then indemnity will be that limit. An example might be a household contents policy where there is a single item limit of £200. Any items of greater value must be specified on the policy or be subject to the lower limit.

Extending indemnity

An insured may sometimes receive more than a strict indemnity.

Reinstatement Memorandum

If a policy is written subject to a Reinstatement Memorandum, then indemnity will be the full reinstatement value at the time of reinstatement without any deductions for depreciation or wear and tear. This cover is paid for by the insured choosing a sum insured that reflects the likely future reinstatement value and therefore paying a greater amount of premium.

New for old cover

This applies to household contents insurance and echoes the intent of the Reinstatement Memorandum described above. In the event of a claim, the insured receives the replacement value of the damaged or lost property at the time of loss, i.e. not subject to the usual deductions for depreciation or wear and tear, so long as the insured items are less than a specified number of years old.

Agreed additional costs

The insured can include the costs associated with the aftermath of a loss (e.g. debris removal, professional fees) within policy cover and be indemnified for these in addition to the amount of the actual loss.

Valued policies

Items of particular value may be insured under a valued or agreed value policy, where the amount to be paid in the event of a total loss is fixed at inception of the policy. Indemnity still operates in the event of a partial loss. Valued policies are common for vintage motor cars, where it is helpful to establish the value of the car at the outset, rather than to try to establish market value at the time of a loss when the vehicle may have been lost or damaged beyond repair.

Subrogation and contribution

SUBROGATION and CONTRIBUTION are often described in insurance as 'corollaries' or natural consequences of indemnity.

Both principles operate to prevent the insured recovering more than indemnity: subrogation to ensure that the insured cannot recover from both his or her insurer and a responsible third party; contribution to ensure that even if there is more than one policy covering the same risk, the insured can recover only the amount that represents indemnity.

Insurable interest

Introduction

An insurance contract can only be legally enforced when the insured has insurable interest in the subject-matter of insurance. To have insurable interest, there must be a legally recognised financial relationship between the insured and the property or event insured, such that the insured would suffer financial loss if the property were destroyed or the insured event happened, or would benefit by the continuing safety of the property or non-occurrence of the event.

How insurable interest arises

Common law recognises an insurable interest where:

* a person owns property;
* a person owes a duty of care towards other people.

Contractual agreements may give one of the parties to the contract certain obligations and consequently create insurable interest. A tenant would not ordinarily be able to insure the property rented because no loss would be suffered if it were damaged. However, if the tenancy contract makes the tenant liable to make good any damage, then the contract gives the tenant insurable interest in the property.

Statutes can also create insurable interest by placing obligations such as the upkeep of property on people, or by granting a benefit.

The Married Women's Property Act 1882 and Married Women's Policies of Assurance (Scotland) Act 1880 (as amended) provide married women with an insurable interest in their own lives and, for their own benefit, in the lives of their husbands.

The Industrial Assurance and Friendly Societies Act 1948 and Amendment Act 1958 allow a person to take out an industrial life policy up to the value of £30 on the life of a parent, step-parent or grandparent. (This was originally intended to cover burial costs.)

Other statutes restrict liability and therefore restrict insurable interest. Examples are:

- the Hotel Proprietors Act 1956, which limits liability for guests' property to £100 per guest in certain circumstances;
- the Carriers' Act 1830, which exempts common carriers from liability exceeding £10 for valuable items unless previously declared;
- the Trustee Act 1925, which entitles trustees to use trust money to insure up to three-quarters of the trust property's value against fire;
- the Carriage of Goods by Sea Act 1971, which limits a carrier's liability to 10,000 gold francs or 30 gold francs per kilo, whichever is higher. This amount can be raised.

Life assurance

A person has unlimited insurable interest:

- in their own life; or
- in the life of their husband or wife.

Insurable interest does not exist in any other family relationships.
    Limited insurable interest exists for:

- partners in each other's lives;
- a creditor in a debtor's life.

Insurable interest exists in these circumstances to the extent of the person's financial interest in the other.

Property insurance

Ownership is the usual relationship that creates insurable interest, but it can arise from other relationships.

- Husband and wife have mutual insurable interest in each other's property.
- An agent may take out insurance on behalf of a principal who has insurable interest.
- A bailee has insurable interest in the goods left in his possession, through his responsibility to take reasonable care of them.
- Trustees and executors of wills have a legal responsibility to look after property which they control. This gives rise to insurable interest.
- Mortgagors (borrowers) and mortgagees (lenders) have insurable interest in the property mortgaged.
- Part or joint owners have insurable interest to the extent of the full value of the property (although they cannot recover more than their own financial interest in the property).

Liability insurance

The amount of insurable interest cannot be established in respect of liability insurance, as the extent of a person's liability is potentially unlimited. Court awards of damages and costs incurred are what determine the extent of most claims and the insured selects a sum insured for the policy which represents the maximum settlement figure foreseeable. Sums insured for large companies may exceed £100 million.

When insurable interest must exist

This varies for different classes of insurance:

- life assurance – when the policy is taken out;
- property and other general insurances – at inception and at time of loss;
- marine insurance – at the time of the loss.

Other features of insurable interest

These are:
- insurable interest cannot be based on a future expectation, such as an inheritance;
- lawful possession of property (with responsibility for its continued safety) creates insurable interest;
- an individual cannot benefit from his or her own criminal acts;
- members of a group can be identified as beneficiaries under a group scheme so long as individual members can be identified at any particular time.

The amount of insurable interest must usually be capable of financial valuation. This requirement doesn't apply to policies on a person's own life or the life of a spouse where interest is considered unlimited. If an employer wishes to effect a policy on an employee's life, the interest must be reasonable and the employer should be able to justify the amount involved.

Insurable risks

Introduction

Insurance is only available in respect of risks which share a range of features that make them insurable.

Features of insurable risks

In order for a risk to be insurable:

- it must be accidental;
- the insured must have a legally recognised financial relationship with the subject-matter of insurance: there must be INSURABLE INTEREST. Only certain relationships are legally recognised as creating insurable interest:

  (a) owners and joint owners of property,

  (b) mortgagees and mortgagors,

  (c) bailees (who hold other people's goods legally),

  (d) agents,

  (e) executors and trustees in respect of property for which they are responsible;

- there must be a sufficient number of exposures to similar risks (homogeneous exposures) in order for the insurer to be able to forecast the expected extent of the loss;
- insuring the risk must not be against public policy, as it is commonly recognised in law that contracts must not go against what society considers the moral course of action;
- the outcome of a risk must be capable of measurement in a financial way;
- it must be 'pure', which means that the only possible outcomes must be either loss or break-even;
- it must be 'particular' arising from an individual cause and affecting individuals, rather than large groups of people.

Uninsurable risks

A number of risks are uninsurable.

- If the outcome of a risk cannot be measured monetarily then it is usually uninsurable. Life assurance is an exception.
- If a risk carries the possibility of loss, break-even or gain, then it is said to be 'speculative'. Such risks are usually undertaken voluntarily and are uninsurable.
- If the risk arises from a cause beyond the control of individuals, has a widespread effect and often causes catastrophic losses, then it is fundamental and uninsurable.

Insurance companies

Introduction

Companies writing insurance can be constituted in various ways, with differing implications for policyholders.

The main forms of insurance companies and their distinguishing features are listed below.

Proprietary companies

Companies:

- formed by registration under the Companies Acts or created by Royal Charter, statute or deed of settlement;
- with authorised and issued share capital;
- whose profits belong to shareholders;
- whose shareholders' liability is limited to the nominal value of their shares;
- with whom business is usually placed using an intermediary.

Mutual companies

Companies:

- formed by deed of settlement or registration under the Companies Acts;
- owned by policyholders;
- whose profits are shared between their policyholders (as lower premiums or higher life assurance bonuses);
- whose policyholders' maximum liability is limited to their premiums or to, at most, an additional £1;
- may transact life or general business;
- cannot issue shares to raise additional capital, hence the movement to demutualisation (i.e. to become a proprietary company).

137

Specialist companies

Companies:

- underwriting only one class of insurance, for example, marine insurance;
- can be either mutual or proprietary.

Composite companies

Companies:

- underwriting several types of business;
- forming the largest part of the insurance market;
- can be either proprietary or mutual.

Direct writing companies

Companies:

- dealing directly with the public and not using intermediaries to place business;
- using the latest in telecommunications to quote on motor, household contents and long-term investment products direct; to complete proposal and claims forms and to issue cover and settle claims.

Industrial life assurance companies

Companies:

- mostly proprietary;
- whose activities are controlled by the Industrial Assurance and Friendly Society Acts;
- which collect premiums weekly or monthly from policyholders.

Collecting friendly societies

Companies:

- run on a mutual basis;
- formed by registration under the Friendly Societies Acts;
- transacting industrial life assurance and sometimes personal accident and sickness insurance;

- mostly operating in a local area rather than nationwide;
- selling small policies providing cover initially for funeral benefits;
- collecting premiums weekly in affordable amounts.

Mutual indemnity associations

Associations:

- originally accepting business only from people who belonged to the same trade and not from members of the general public;
- which have subsequently mostly been re-formed into mutual or proprietary companies accepting business from anyone.

Captive insurance companies

Companies:

- set up as subsidiaries by parent companies to underwrite some insurable risks in a tax-efficient manner;
- enable parent companies to pay premiums based on their own experience rather than shared experience with other risks;
- enjoy lower premiums because of lack of need to produce profit, and to cover operating expenses of insurer;
- access reinsurance at lower costs than could a commercial market insurer;
- enable premiums to be offset against corporation tax;
- often operated from offshore sites with tax and administrative advantages.

Reinsurance companies

Companies:

- which specialise in transferring risk from insurance companies. Risks are accepted by the insurance company, which then passes on to the reinsurer any proportion of the potential loss that it does not wish to bear itself.

Insurance Companies Act 1982

Introduction

Regulation of the insurance industry is for the most part achieved by the Insurance Companies Act 1982 as amended by the Insurance (Third Insurance Directive) Regulations 1994 (but see also Financial Services Act 1986), in addition to the various general Companies Acts.

The Act has 100 sections, grouped into five main Parts, dealing with:

Part 1 – restrictions on carrying out insurance business;

Part 2 – the regulation of insurance companies;

Part 3 – the conduct of insurance business;

Part 4 – special classes of insurers;

Part 5 – supplementary issues.

Part 1

This defines the 18 classes of general insurance business and the nine classes of long-term business. It also sets out the requirements that must be met by anyone wishing to gain authorisation to write insurance business in the United Kingdom.

Authorisation

The responsibility for authorising insurance companies in the UK lies with the Secretary of State for Trade and Industry (now also known as the President of the Board of Trade), who needs detailed information about a company and the people involved in running it before a decision can be made. Each EU member state is responsible for authorising its own companies.

A company may be authorised to carry on a particular class of business, or parts of a class, but apart from long-term business and/or reinsurance cannot be authorised to write both long-term and general business.

There are different authorisation requirements for companies with head offices in the UK, in other EU member states or outside the EU.

United Kingdom

The company must:

- be a company as defined under the Companies Acts; or
- be a registered society or corporate body defined under charter or statute and already be authorised for other insurance business;
- not have any not fully paid up share capital issued after 1 January 1983; and
- the director, controller, manager or main agent of the applicant company must appear to the Secretary of State to be a fit and proper person for his position.

Other EU member states

The company must:

- have a suitable representative who is resident in the UK and who, to the Secretary of State, appears to be a fit and proper person for his position;
- satisfy the Secretary of State that it is authorised to transact insurance in its own state if it wishes to be authorised to write reinsurance in the UK.

Outside EU

The company must:

- be entitled by the law in the state where its head office is located to transact long-term or general insurance;
- have the prescribed value of UK assets and have deposited this amount with the required person;
- have a suitable representative who is resident in the UK and who, to the Secretary of State, appears to be a fit and proper person for his position.

The Secretary of State must be given notice of the appointment of certain officers and of changes to them, so that prior approval for the appointment or change can be given.

Insurance Companies (Third Insurance Directive) Regulations 1994

These regulations implement the Third EC Non-life and Life Insurance Directives.

The objective of the directives is for a single licence to permit life and non-life companies to sell their full range of products across the European Community.

The directives set out detailed harmonisation requirements on technical reserves, matching and localisation of assets, solvency margins and control management.

Part 2

This identifies the annual accounts that must be submitted to the Department of Trade and Industry (DTI), the actuarial investigations that may be undertaken and the ways in which insurance companies may be wound up.

The Secretary of State has the power to intervene in an insurance company's affairs to stop particular investments being made; to require the value of assets to be retained in the UK or limit premiums; to impose actuarial investigations or to require companies to provide a more detailed or faster supply of accounting information. He or she can order the company to take any action needed to protect policyholders' interests.

Accounts statements

The Insurance Company (Accounts and Statement) Regulations 1983 set out the precise form in which annual insurance returns must be made and their contents.

Every insurance company, every financial year, must prepare a revenue account, a balance sheet and a profit and loss account (or an income and expenditure account for non-profit organisations).

Composite insurance companies must keep all assets from long-term business separate from those from general business and separate solvency margins apply and must be maintained by both funds. Proprietary companies must keep shareholders' funds (on which solvency margins are based) separate from their own insurance business assets.

Any company authorised to write long-term business must appoint an actuary who must value the long-term fund once a year.

Account submission

Accounts must be audited and submitted to the DTI within six months of the end of the financial year concerned. Their purpose is to demonstrate the insurer's solvency and to enable the soundness of its reserving policies to be checked. The forms issued by the DTI must be followed precisely.

The 18 general business authorisation classes are divided into ten accounting classes for returns. Insurance companies must prepare separate forms in respect of premiums and claims for each accounting class of business carried on, subdivided by the country where business was done, by risk group and by currency.

All companies are required to submit:

- a balance sheet;
- a profit and loss account;
- a certificate from the company's directors and auditors.

For general business, a revenue account and information about major reinsurances must also be submitted.

For long-term business, an actuary's report and a statement of ordinary long-term business are required.

Newly authorised companies have special requirements imposed on them so that their activities can be scrutinised by the DTI.

Solvency margins

The solvency margin is the minimum amount by which the assets of a company must exceed its liabilities. The concept was introduced by the Assurance Companies Act 1946.

The solvency requirements differ according to where the head office of the insurance company is based: in the UK, in another member state or outside the EU.

There are specific margins imposed on general and long-term insurance business that reflect those required by EU directives and are monitored by the Department of Trade and Industry. The type of business being written determines the margin by which assets must exceed liabilities.

The EU has set a minimum margin, the 'minimum guarantee fund', which is a fixed sum in European Currency Units set at different levels for different types of insurance companies.

The Policyholders Protection Board, set up under the Policyholders Protection Act 1975, can impose a levy on all authorised insurance companies to raise funds that can then become available if an insurer is unable to meet its liabilities to its policyholders through insolvency.

Winding up

The Secretary of State can petition the courts for an insurance company to be wound up if:

- it is unable to pay its debts;
- it does not comply with a requirement of the Insurance Companies Act 1982; or
- it fails to produce or to keep proper accounting records.

A company can also be wound up by the courts at the petition of ten or more policyholders whose policies' total value exceeds £10,000.

Part 3

This deals with the manner in which insurance companies conduct business: the use of advertisements, the issue of cooling-off notices in respect of long-term insurance contracts and disclosure by intermediaries of their connections with insurance companies.

Part 4

This relates to Lloyd's of London and to industrial life companies, which, together with trades union/employers associations are exempt from the authorisation requirements of the Act. It also relates to non-UK companies.

Part 5

This sets out the criminal proceedings that may follow any breach of the Act.

Insurance Ombudsman Bureau

Introduction

The IOB was set up in 1981 to be an entirely independent way for insurance disputes to be settled.

Operation of the IOB

The Ombudsman can only handle disputes relating to personal insurances. Commercial disputes are settled at arbitration where policies carry this condition, or in the courts as a matter of last resort.

Although insureds only have recourse to the IOB scheme if their insurer is a member of it, Lloyd's of London and over 350 insurance companies are now members, representing over 90% of all personal insurance business underwritten.

The Ombudsman will only become involved in a dispute once all other steps to resolution have failed. Before being considered by the Ombudsman, cases must have been referred to the senior management of the company concerned. If the insured is not satisfied with the response from the company's senior management, and wishes the case to be passed to the Ombudsman, this must be done within six months of the response being received.

The Ombudsman's decision is binding on the insurance company, which must pay the monetary award imposed, up to a maximum limit. However, the insured can choose whether or not to accept the decision, or to pursue the issue through the courts.

Personal Insurance Arbitration Service

The PIAS is a scheme set up and administered by the Chartered Institute of Arbitrators and provides a mechanism for disputes to be settled in personal insurance cases without recourse to the Insurance Ombudsman.

The appointment of the arbitrator is entirely independent of the insurer, even though the insurer must pay the arbitrator's fee even if the decision is made in the insured's favour. Both insurer and insured are bound to accept the decision of the arbitrator.

Intermediaries

Introduction

In the insurance market intermediaries are responsible for bringing together those who wish to buy insurance and those who offer insurance. There are three main types of intermediary:

- insurance brokers (including Lloyd's brokers);

- agents;

- advisers/consultants.

Insurance brokers

The Insurance Brokers Registration Act 1977 made it an offence for anyone to use the term 'insurance broker' without being registered with the body set up to monitor the registration of brokers, the Insurance Brokers Registration Council. The IBRC requires those who wish to be registered to meet certain criteria which relate to qualifications, experience, accounting and professional indemnity insurance. The title 'insurance broker' is therefore a useful indication of a company having a fair amount of expertise and operating to professional standards.

A broker will have access to a very wide range of companies with which to place business and will often also be able to assist clients with risk assessment and control.

Lloyd's brokers

In order to be able to place business with syndicates at Lloyd's of London, a broker must satisfy the Committee of Lloyd's of its experience, integrity and financial standing in the market, in addition to meeting any IBRC requirements. Only Lloyd's brokers are allowed to place business at Lloyd's, although some Lloyd's brokers have arrangements to place business on behalf of non-Lloyd's brokers. The inclusion of the phrase 'at Lloyd's' on a broker's stationery is a further indication of its professional standing.

Agents

Insurance agents are not normally employed full time as insurance intermediaries, but instead have full-time occupations which involve giving advice and placing insurance occasionally, such as solicitors or estate agents.

An agent may hold up to six agencies, but will be limited to recommending the products of those companies only.

Tied agents

Tied agents are found in the life assurance market. A tied agent represents a single company and may only sell that company's products. The term 'tied agent' usually refers to a company (such as a building society linked to a particular insurer) and the term 'company representative' is used for the people who work for the tied agent. These in turn may only sell the products of the company to which their employer is tied. The industrial/ordinary branch life assurance offices still employ people who are empowered to sell only their own company's products.

Advisers/consultants

Intermediaries who place general insurances as a full-time occupation, but who have not registered with the IBRC and agreed to abide by its regulatory requirements, often call themselves insurance consultants, or insurance advisers. They may have access to the same markets as brokers, but not follow the same accounting practices or hold the same professional indemnity insurance.

Independent financial advisers

In the financial services industry, IFAs offer access to life and investment products from a wide range of providers. Brokers providing advice on investment products are regulated by the IBRC. The activities of IFAs are regulated by the Personal Investment Authority, which requires them to put clients' interests ahead of their own, to know their clients' personal and financial situations before giving advice and to recommend financial products that are most suitable for their clients' needs.

Key person insurance

Introduction

The death or long-term disability of a person who is key to a company's profitability, such as a director, a top sales person or a designer, can have a detrimental impact on a company. Key person insurance is a form of business interruption insurance that attempts to replace the company's losses through the absence of the key person.

Cover

LIFE ASSURANCE cover on a term or whole life basis can be arranged to cover the death risk, while a CRITICAL ILLNESS INSURANCE or PERMANENT HEALTH INSURANCE policy would cover the disability risk.

Sum insured

Calculating the appropriate sum insured is difficult, as it is not possible to quantify exactly what the company's financial loss will be in the event of the key person's absence.

Two methods are used:

- a chosen multiplier is applied to the key person's gross remuneration (this is known as the rule of thumb method);
- the company's gross profits are multiplied by the key person's remuneration and this figure is then divided by the company's total wage bill. The result is then multiplied by the number of years that cover is intended to last.

Financial underwriting is needed to check that the amounts are reasonable in the light of the company's past performance.

Risk assessment

The company employing the key person is assured under the policy, so the underwriter will look in detail at its operations, and at the duties and expertise of the key person in order to establish the amount of its insurable interest in the key person.

Legal expenses insurance

Introduction

Legal expenses insurance will reimburse a policyholder for expenses related to defending or pursuing a range of legal actions.

Although this guide looks at the commercial policy, cover can be provided for individuals and families, although this is usually done as an extension to a household contents or a private motor insurance policy.

Policy cover

Although there is no standard policy cover for legal expenses insurance, policies commonly offer cover for costs incurred in:

- taking legal action to enforce legal rights against third parties;
- resolving disputes related to contracts;
- defending a civil claim or criminal action (no fines or penalties can be covered as this would be against public policy).

Loss assessors' fees following a disputed insurance claim are covered if the claim exceeds £2,500.

Jury service allowance of £150 per individual per day, up to a total of £10,000 in any one year is provided.

In addition to a specified maximum limit of indemnity for any one claim (say £50,000 to £250,000), policies usually specify an aggregate limit (say £1 million) – this means that each claim made within the period of insurance will reduce the total limit of indemnity that remains available to the insured for the rest of the policy term.

They are also written on a claims made basis, covering only losses notified to the insurer during the period of insurance and excluding any acts prior to inception of the policy which the insured should have known were likely to give rise to a claim.

Excesses are also common, related to a percentage of the claim rather than a fixed sum.

Advisory services are a feature of legal expenses insurance, providing 24-hour advice to policyholders on a range of legal questions.

Checklist: Types of cover

A company may be faced with many legal problems and a typical policy will address these under the headings of:

- employment disputes;
- property;
- contracts;
- criminal prosecutions;
- patents, registered designs, copyright and trade marks;
- motor vehicles;
- Inland Revenue investigations and VAT tribunals;
- Data Protection Act 1984;
- special risks.

Employment disputes

Covered:

- costs of fees, expenses and witnesses' attendance at Tribunal and County Court hearings or other legal proceedings arising from an action by an employee or ex-employee under employment legislation;
- awards of compensation under statutes and statutory instruments relating to employees' rights and conditions of work.

Not covered:

- personal injury or property damage risks which should be covered by employer's or public liability policies.

Property disputes

Covered:

- costs of pursuit or defence of civil actions and for representatives of the company to attend the hearings;
- costs arising from the negligence of a third party whilst on the insured's premises.

Not covered:

- actions relating to goods in transit or hired to third parties, or goods on premises not usually occupied by the insured.

Contract disputes

Covered:

- fees and expenses of legal proceedings relating to disputes between the insured and a customer or a supplier in respect of the purchase or supply of goods or services;
- costs awarded against the insured in respect of such disputes.

Not covered:

- undisputed debt recovery fees (though policy can be extended to provide this cover);
- claims of less than £500;
- lease or tenancy matters;
- vehicle-related disputes;
- contract of employment disputes.

Criminal prosecution

Covered:

- costs of defending criminal prosecutions against the company, its directors, or employees who are pension scheme trustees under various pieces of legislation such as the Health and Safety at Work etc. Act 1974, the Companies Acts and the Consumer Protection Act 1987;
- fees and expenses including witnesses' expenses.

Not covered:

- fines or penalties imposed.

Patents, registered designs, copyright, trademarks

Covered:

- legal fees and expenses incurred in pursuing actions against infringement of industrial or intellectual property rights;
- defence costs against an action alleging infringement of another's policy.

Motor vehicle disputes

Covered:

- disputes relating to the servicing or supply of motor vehicles;
- defence of the insured and employees against prosecutions for motoring offences;
- expenses involved in applications for removal of driving licence disqualifications;
- fees and expenses incurred to recover uninsured losses resulting from a road traffic accident.

Not covered:

- fines or penalties imposed as a result of prosecutions for road traffic offences.

Inland Revenue investigations and VAT tribunals

Covered:

- fees and expenses of legal representation, including accountants' fees.

Not covered:

- claims where accounts returns have not been properly maintained and submitted to the tax authorities.

Data Protection Act 1984

Covered:

- the cost of defending actions brought under the Data Protection Act against the company as a data user, in the event of unauthorised disclosure, loss or retention of inaccurate information;
- payment of compensation awards to data subjects.

Special risks

Covers risks not normally accommodated, such as:

- investigations by trade or professional associations;
- costs of public enquiries;
- statutory licence protection;
- wrongful arrest proceedings;
- breach of covenant proceedings.

Policy exclusions

Those common to liability polices generally:

- war, riot and civil commotion;
- radioactive contamination;
- more specific insurances;
- claims beyond specified territorial limits;
- acts, omissions or disputes before inception of policy if insured knew or should have known of them;
- court-imposed fines or penalties.

Those that should be covered by other policies:

- employer's liability and public liability risks.

Those specific to legal expenses insurance:

- mining, subsidence or heave disputes;
- disputes involving goods in transit, lent or hired to third parties or at premises not occupied by the insured (unless related to work being done by the insured or to installation);
- representation during taxation proceedings if the insured has made an intentionally misleading misstatement.

Policy conditions

Those related to general liability policies:

- premium adjustment;
- fraudulent claims;
- observance of policy terms and conditions;
- claims notification;
- cancellation;
- measures to be taken to avoid losses.

Those specific to legal expenses policies:

- the insured must take reasonable care to keep business records and submit tax returns when required;
- claims will only be met if there are good grounds for pursuing or defending a claim or proceedings and if necessary opinion of counsel will be sought to confirm this;
- if the insured is insolvent the insurers may withdraw support on a claim;
- the insured can appoint its own legal representative if this person is acceptable to the insurer;

- the insurer has the final decision on whether a claim is admissible and whether to withdraw support following the insured's rejection of a claim settlement, but other disputes will be referred to arbitration by a solicitor or a barrister.

Underwriting

Information about the risk will be sought using a proposal form. The name, address, business details and length of time that the business has been established are relevant, as is the turnover and estimated turnover for the next year and the number of employees and their remuneration.

For cover against prosecutions under the Data Protection Act 1984, more specific information will be required about registration, about the purpose for which data is held and about the systems that exist for managing the data and keeping it secure.

Of vital importance will be any information relating to past claims and to any claims which the proposer thinks may be outstanding.

Rating

A rate applies to turnover or to the number of employees and depends on the type of cover wanted by the insured and the type of business in which the insured is engaged.

Co-insurance

The insured may have to pay 10% of each claim settled against it, but will be able to recover all costs for cases that are successful.

Libel and slander insurance

Introduction

This form of insurance is also known as defamation insurance, as libel and slander are both torts of defamation. In order to defame a person, a statement made about them must expose them to hatred, ridicule, contempt or fear and in so doing injure their reputation or their professional standing. It is important for the person to have a reputation that can be injured – merely to hurt their dignity or feelings does not constitute defamation.

Libel is a defamatory statement that is in a permanent form and normally published; slander is defamation in a transient form and is normally spoken. Both forms of defamation must involve a third party to whom the statement is published, and publishing in this context means hearing, seeing or reading the statement.

Checklist: Forms of libel and slander

Libel

- written documents;
- printed documents;
- pictures;
- sculptures;
- advertising posters;
- cartoons;
- radio or television broadcasts.

Slander

- spoken words;
- gestures.

Innocent defamation

If the words were not intended to be defamatory, the person who published them may offer to publish a suitable correction and apology and to try to notify this to those persons who had received the defamatory publication. Under the Defamation Act 1952, this relieves the innocent publisher of further liability.

Identification

In order for a court to accept that a statement is defamatory, it must be shown that the people to whom the statement was published understood it to refer to the person claiming defamation. If this is so, then there is defamation.

A statement about a group of people can be defamatory if the group is sufficiently small for the reputations of the people in the group to suffer. So, if a statement was made about the supporters of a particular club, it would not be possible to claim defamation, but if made about a small group of the club's directors then defamation would be possible.

Proving defamation

Libel is said to be actionable *per se*, meaning 'in itself'. If a statement capable of injuring a person's reputation is published in a permanent form to a third party, then the person defamed has the right to recover damages whether or not their reputation has actually suffered.

Slander requires the defamed person to prove that their reputation has been damaged, unless the statement:

- alleges that the person has committed a crime for which the punishment is death or imprisonment;
- implies that a woman has been unchaste;
- disparages a person in respect of their profession or business;
- alleges that the person has a disease that is contagious or infectious.

Defamation cases are currently heard by a jury, which recommends the amount of the award to be made to a successful plaintiff. Awards can therefore be extremely high.

Defamation policy

Defamation cover can be provided by a separate policy or written as an extension to a PROFESSIONAL INDEMNITY INSURANCE policy. Cover is provided to the insured, which includes directors, employees or other officials of the insured company.

Professional indemnity extension

The professional indemnity policy extension will provide cover on a claims made basis for any alleged libel, slander or other injurious falsehood published by the insured in its professional capacity, but not if published in a journal, magazine or newspaper or through the medium of radio or television. There is likely to be a limit of indemnity of perhaps £10,000, or a percentage of the total professional indemnity policy indemnity limit.

Policy cover

There is no standard policy wording, but most policies will indemnify the insured against losses (legal liability for damages, claimant's costs and expenses; costs of withdrawing a publication containing a defamatory statement; other costs incurred by, or with the written consent of, the company) related to claims made during the period of insurance for:

- libel, injurious falsehood or slander of title or of goods;
- passing off or infringement of trademark, patent right, copyright or registered design in a specified publication;
- slander that the insured has committed in the course of its business.

Losses in any one period of insurance are subject to a specified limit of indemnity, with the insured also being required to cover a fixed percentage of every claim (often 10%).

Exclusions

The defamation policy specifically excludes:

- criminal libel;
- any loss resulting from personal ill-will of the insured toward the person defamed;
- actions for damages outside the UK;
- liability arising because of the existence of some agreement;
- losses relating to computer software.

Policy conditions

The policy will include a QC clause, which releases the insurer from defending actions unless in the opinion of a Queen's Counsel the action would have a reasonable chance of success. If the insurer does not defend a case, the insured must do whatever the insurer requires of it, in apologising or withdrawing a publication, to achieve settlement of the claim.

Another condition requires the insured to involve the insurers in any decision to publish what the insured recognises may be contentious material.

Life assurance

Introduction

This is a very large subject and beyond the scope of this guide. The Financial Services Act 1986 imposes very strict requirements on anyone giving advice on what, under the terms of the Act, are investment products – essentially any contract that allows for the possibility of a gain being made. Product providers and intermediaries are subject to the Personal Investment Authority Code of Conduct. In selecting products of this kind it is essential to check on the quality of advice being given.

Outlined below are some of the more basic forms of cover.

Term assurance

A term assurance policy pays out the sum assured on the death of the life assured during the term of the policy. If the life assured does not die during the term of the policy then no sum assured is paid and no premiums are returned. For this reason, term assurance is relatively cheap. The assured chooses a sum assured equal to the amount of cover required and specifies the term. The amount of the premium depends on the amount of the sum assured, the age of the proposed life assured and the length of the term.

Whole of life assurance

A whole of life assurance policy (now usually known as a 'whole life' assurance policy) provides life cover for the duration of the life assured's life, not just for a fixed term. Premium payments remain level throughout the period of cover, being calculated from the age of the life assured at the inception of the policy and the amount of the sum assured. Premium payments may cease when the assured reaches a particular age (say, 60 or 65). As in term assurance, the sum assured will have to be paid at some time. Consequently the assurer must invest premiums well in order to ensure that sufficient funds are available to meet the eventual claim.

With-profit policies

Some whole life policies can share in any profit made by the assurance company from its investments, in return for a higher premium payment. Such policies are known as 'with-profit' policies (as opposed to 'without-profit' policies which pay out just the sum assured specified in the policy). In with-profit policies, the share of the profit takes the form of a bonus added to the sum assured.

Bonuses can take one of three forms:

Reversionary bonuses: are usually declared each year as a percentage of the sum assured, with the bonus being added to the original sum assured. In subsequent years the bonus would be calculated on the original sum assured plus any bonuses that had already been added to it. The policy guarantees to pay any reversionary bonuses that have been declared.

Terminal bonuses: are calculated at the date of claim and are not guaranteed in advance.

Interim bonuses: declare what bonus rate will apply to any claims that arise between the last bonus declaration and the next one due.

Endowment assurance

Endowment policies are designed to pay out the sum assured (plus bonuses if the policy is written on a with-profit basis) at the end of a specified period or on the earlier death of the life assured. Premiums paid depend on the size of the sum assured, the age of the life assured at the start of the policy and the length of the term.

Endowment assurance policies have a strong investment element as payment of the sum assured is guaranteed at a fixed future date or on the assured's earlier death. They can only be sold subject to the requirements of the Financial Services Act 1986 being met.

Endowments are often used in conjunction with an interest-only mortgage, as some means of ensuring that there is sufficient capital available to pay off the loan at the end of the loan period if necessary. This is the role of the endowment policy. A policy is written to mature at the same time as the mortgage is due to be repaid, with a sum assured that is the same as the capital outstanding on the mortgage. During the term of the mortgage, the interest on the loan is paid each month to the lender, and premiums are paid regularly to the life assurance company in respect of the endowment assurance. The policy is assigned to the lender, so that in the event of the assured's death, the lender would receive full repayment of the loan.

At the end of the mortgage term, all the interest on the loan has been repaid and the endowment policy matures to pay off the capital debt.

If the endowment policy has been written on a with-profit basis, then any surplus left after the mortgage capital has been repaid may be retained by the assured.

Low cost endowments

In a low cost endowment policy, the sum assured chosen is substantially less than would be required to repay the loan. Instead the addition of bonuses over the period of the policy is relied upon to bring the initial sum assured up to the level required to repay the loan on maturity. Premiums for this type of cover are therefore lower than for policies where the sum assured represents the amount needed at maturity from the outset. The death benefit under the policy will always be enough to repay the loan.

Low cost low start endowments

A low cost low start endowment works on the same principle, but holds premiums at a lower level for the first few years of the policy. Premiums will rise each year during this time, until the proper level is reached. As with the low cost endowment, the death benefit under the policy will always be enough to repay the loan. This type of policy has advantages in that lower premiums are paid during the first few years of the policy and cheaper policy cover is provided as the full sum assured is not guaranteed from the outset.

However, there are also disadvantages, as the assured may find it difficult to afford the increases in the premiums over the first few years of the policy and, more worryingly, the sum assured may not be sufficient to repay the loan at maturity if the life company's investments do not perform to expectations over the period of the policy and bonuses do not accrue at the levels needed to bring the sum assured to the required level.

Industrial life assurance (home service insurance)

This originated to meet the needs of workers in the industrial revolution for policies that could be funded by small contributions collected weekly from their homes, and which were designed to cover little more than funeral costs.

Industrial life assurance companies now also write ordinary life assurance policies, but may still make arrangements to collect premiums regularly from policyholders.

Unit trusts

Policyholders can choose to take out unit trust policies, where units in a life assurance investment fund are allocated to them and the returns on these units contribute towards the surrender and maturity values. As the units are linked to the value of the assets bought for the life investment fund, there is a possibility that the value of the units could go down, rather than up. The risk of this type of policy is higher, but then again, so are the potential rewards.

Checklist: Life assurance terminology

Actuary: a person concerned with the application of probability and statistical theory to problems of insurance, investment, financial management and demography. Plays a critical role in the annual evaluation of assets and liabilities of insurance companies to ensure that these meet the solvency requirements of the DTI.

Assignment: to transfer an interest or right under a policy from one person to another.

Loan: life offices will often make a loan available against the security of a policy (not a term or unit trust policy) up to 90% of the surrender value. Interest rates reflect market conditions. The policyholder promises to repay the loan, plus interest, and to continue to pay the premiums. Any amount not repaid when the policy matures is deducted from the payment at maturity.

Paid-up policy: if a policyholder can't afford to pay further premiums, he or she can ask for the policy to be made 'paid-up'. Premiums cease to be payable, but cover continues at a reduced rate. This applies only to whole life and endowment policies.

Surrender value: if a policy is cashed in before it becomes a claim, it is 'surrendered' and there may be a small return on premiums paid. Although accrued bonuses can be included, a surrender value is usually significantly less than premiums paid in, because of acquisition and administrative costs that will be deducted. The earlier a policy is surrendered, the smaller the value – in the first few years there may be no value at all.

Group life assurance

Life assurance can be written on a group basis, to provide cover on improved terms for an identifiable group of people, such as a company's employees or the members of a club.

Rather than writing many individual policies, a master policy providing cover for all members of the group is likely to be used. Each member of the group will receive his or her own certificate confirming cover and scheme membership. Premium contributions can be made by an employer on behalf of scheme members, or by the individuals themselves, in which case they will also receive a copy of the rules that apply to the scheme.

The master policy will probably be accompanied by two schedules, setting out the scheme details and any conditions that apply.

Schedule 1

This will include information on the company name in which the master policy is to be issued, the commencement date for the scheme and details of the normal retirement age for members of the scheme.

It will set out who may join the scheme (usually anyone who applies, or anyone who is actively at work on a set date), the scheme salary (the basic annual salary paid to each life assured at the last anniversary of the commencement date), the sum assured (x times the scheme salary), to whom benefits should be paid (head office in trust is usual under a master policy) and set out the amount of free cover (a financial amount for the sum assured, below which the applicant does not need to provide any medical or other lifestyle evidence).

Schedule 2

The following conditions are likely to apply:

- full medical details must be provided for each applicant when they join the scheme and if they wish to increase the sum assured;
- evidence of the life assured's age must be given to the insurance company before any claim will be paid;
- the company may require proof of the happening of the insured event;
- if premiums are not paid within 31 days of renewal, cover will cease;
- proportionate refunds may be given to scheme members who leave the company's employment before cover under the scheme expires;
- the opportunity to take out insurance at favourable terms may be given to scheme members who leave the company and go to work elsewhere;
- benefits under the policy will not be transferable to a third party as they are payable at the discretion of the scheme trustee (the company running the scheme).

Rating

The underwriter will consider the likely claims experience of the group as a whole and only underwrite individual lives where benefits are higher than those provided within free cover limits.

Checklist: Details required for group life scheme

- Number of lives in the company.
- Number of lives in the scheme.
- The business of the company and any processes involved.
- The potential for catastrophe claims.
- The numbers of workers engaged in manual as opposed to sedentary occupations.
- Previous scheme claims experience.
- The level of benefits that the scheme is to provide.
- The age at which membership of the scheme must cease.
- The split between male and female workers.
- The geographical location of the company and of workers within it.

Lloyd's of London

Introduction

Lloyd's of London had its origins in the 17th century, when those wishing to share in insurance on marine risks chose a café belonging to Edward Lloyd as their meeting place. Lloyd encouraged his clients by providing them with information about insurance and shipping as well as a conducive atmosphere in which to do business.

Lloyd's today acts in much the same way, as a meeting place for those engaged in transacting insurance where information on insurance is available in a number of specialised publications.

Underwriting members

Lloyd's is not an insurance company, but a market in which individuals can band together to accept risks. Insurances at Lloyd's are placed with underwriting members known as 'names', who accept risks within the four principal classes of business: marine, non-marine, aviation and motor.

Names accept business solely on their own account and thus have an individual liability for losses in respect of any risks that they accept. This individual liability is unlimited and a call can be made upon their entire personal wealth if necessary, to meet a liability to an insured.

Before prospective names can be accepted, they must provide independent verification of a minimum level of readily realisable assets (known as their qualifying means). It is assumed that their actual wealth significantly exceeds this figure. The level of funds required will depend on the class of business underwritten and the syndicates chosen, with higher levels of funds required for more volatile business.

In order to limit the liability of individual names, following the instances of hardship caused by calls on some names in recent times, they are now allowed to underwrite through limited liability companies.

In addition to the private individuals who are names, Lloyd's has accepted corporate names since 1994, in order to attract new investment into the market. These corporate members have limited liability for losses.

Syndicates

A syndicate is a group of names who have delegated their underwriting authority to a professional underwriter, who in turn is supported by clerical staff.

Each name at Lloyd's joins one or more underwriting syndicates and accepts a percentage commitment of the risks underwritten by the syndicate. The syndicate is limited in the risks that it can accept, by the total premium income limit of its members, which is what is meant by its underwriting 'capacity'.

Policy security

Lloyd's sets great store by the security of its promise to indemnify insureds and has put the following systems in place to ensure that funds are always available to meet claims:

- premiums are paid into a trust fund from which only claims, underwriting expenses and reinsurance premiums can be paid (Lloyd's has a three-year accounting system which means that profits cannot be taken until three years have elapsed since the business was written);
- members must deposit assets in a trust fund in proportion to their premium income limit (set by Lloyd's): individuals are required to deposit 20% to 50% of their premium income limit, corporate members 50% but with a minimum deposit of £1.5 million;
- each individual must show a minimum level of personal wealth of £250,000;
- all members must pay an annual contribution into the New Central Fund which would be drawn upon in the event of a member being unable to meet their underwriting liabilities. This requirement applies both to individual and to corporate names.

Placing business at Lloyd's

Business is brought to Lloyd's by insurance brokers who have been required to satisfy Lloyd's of their financial standing and integrity (see INTERMEDIARIES) and who agree to abide by the extensive Code of Practice for Lloyd's Brokers. Private motor business and personal lines business such as household insurance can now be brought to Lloyd's without having to go via a Lloyd's broker.

In place of PROPOSAL FORMS, slips are used to provide details of risks. Increasingly, risks are being placed electronically, using the Electronic Placing and Support (EPS) system.

A policy is prepared in accordance with the information on the slip and then sent to Lloyd's Policy Signing Office for checking and signature on behalf of all the syndicates that have accepted a share in the risk.

Statutory regulation of Lloyd's

Lloyd's has had its own constitution since the Lloyd's Act 1871, which made it an incorporated society and gave it the power to make byelaws, under which it regulates its own affairs. Nevertheless, it is still subject to the INSURANCE COMPANIES ACT 1982 in three main areas.

Premiums trust fund

Underwriters are required to pay all premiums into a trust fund out of which claims and underwriting expenses are met. Profits can be distributed from the fund only after three years, in line with Lloyd's three-year accounting system.

Solvency test

Every underwriting member of Lloyd's must annually submit to a solvency test conducted by a qualified accountant approved by the Council of Lloyd's in order to confirm that the member's assets at Lloyd's are sufficient to meet their underwriting liabilities. Any necessary additional funds must be provided or the member must cease underwriting. The requirements of the solvency test must be approved by the Department of Trade and Industry.

Every member of Lloyd's must have sufficient assets; otherwise Lloyd's will be deemed to be insolvent. With effect from 31 December 1997, each member's assets also have to be sufficient to meet a solvency margin of 16% of annual premium income or 23% of average claims over a three-year period.

Statement of business/global accounts

This statutory statement of the underwriting results and solvency of the entire Lloyd's market must be filed annually with the Secretary of State for Trade and Industry.

Self-regulation at Lloyd's

This is controlled by the Council of Lloyd's, which is made up of 18 members: six working members (actively working in Lloyd's affairs), six external members (not actively working in Lloyd's affairs – this includes corporate members) and six nominated members appointed by the Council and their appointments confirmed by the Governor of the Bank of England.

Council makes or revokes byelaws that regulate Lloyd's activities and operates a disciplinary system.

In addition to the Council of Lloyd's, regulation is achieved through the existence of a **Market Board** (which sets minimum standards in areas relating to the reputation, efficiency and cost-effectiveness of the market and agrees those standards of conduct that should apply to all types of business written by Lloyd's) and a **Regulatory Board** (which provides and administers a set of rules that protect the interests of Lloyd's members while upholding their contractual obligations to policyholders and others and meeting the legal requirements of the countries in which they do business).

Corporation of Lloyd's

The Corporation of Lloyd's provides the premises, services and assistance necessary for the conduct of underwriting and for the regulation of the market.

Long-term care insurance

Introduction

This provides benefits to individuals who become unable to care for themselves without external assistance and is usually associated with the elderly.

Policy cover

Two policy options exist:

- fee care plans for residents in nursing homes or residential accommodation;
- benefits if an individual cannot meet a specified number of criteria used to gauge disability.

Fee care plans

An annuity is bought for a lump sum payment and payments are then made direct to the home involved in the care of the dependent person.

The annuity cover can be arranged in various ways, all of which involve some degree of return of capital for early death.

Disability benefits

If the insured becomes unable to perform a specific number of activities of daily living (ADLs) then disability benefits are paid after a certain period of disability.

Activities of daily living:

- getting into or out of a chair or bed;
- dressing unaided;
- going to the toilet;
- washing;
- eating and drinking unaided.

Benefits can either be payable for life, or paid until a personal trust fund is exhausted. They can increase as it becomes impossible for the person to accomplish more ADLs and include care at home, respite care or a contribution towards nursing home fees.

Exclusions

The policy excludes:

- self-inflicted injury;
- war risks;
- failure to follow medical advice;
- AIDS or HIV.

Loss adjusters and assessors

Introduction

Insurers use the services of Chartered Loss Adjusters, independent and professionally qualified people who assist in the investigation, negotiation and settlement of claims and provide other loss-related services.

Loss adjusters

Loss adjusters are experts in dealing with claims and will follow a claim through from first intimation to the insurer to settlement, ensuring that as far as possible further loss is minimised and reporting to the insurer on the circumstances of the loss, the adequacy of the sum insured at the time of the loss, investigating any unusual circumstances and generally bringing about the settlement of the claim as quickly as possible.

Although employed by the insurer, they can also be of great help to the insured in providing advice and guidance on the best steps to be taken following a loss.

Checklist: Report contents

A full report prepared by a loss adjuster for an insurer would include information under the following headings:

* description of premises and of business carried on;
* discovery of incident;
* cause and extent of damage and how damage was stopped;
* initial measures taken to protect premises;
* whether insured has complied with any warranties;
* possible rights of recovery against third party;
* recommended amount insurers should reserve (allocate) for settlement of the claim;
* details of the claim and any adjustments made;

- adequacy of sums insured;
- salvage;
- other insurances;
- payment details.

Loss assessors

Loss assessors are normally employed by the insured to assist in the settlement of a claim. Their fees are paid by the insured and may not form part of the claim. No set fee scales exist. Fees would be negotiated on the basis of the likely work involved in assessing a particular claim.

The expertise that an assessor may bring to a claim can be very useful to an insured who is facing difficult decisions at a traumatic time. The assessor helps the insured to prepare information about the claim for presentation to the insurer, and will represent the insured in negotiating a claim settlement.

Assessors may be used by smaller companies and Lloyd's syndicates to assist in the settlement of liability claims.

Loss Prevention Council

Introduction

The Loss Prevention Council comprises the following organisations, each with different functions:

- Loss Prevention Certification Board;

- Fire Protection Association;

- Loss Prevention Council Technical Centre;

- National Approval Council for Security Systems.

Loss Prevention Certification Board

This develops and operates quality assurance schemes for fire and security products and services, providing independent, objective assessment of integrity, performance, manufacturing quality and installation of all types of loss prevention products and services.

Quality assurance schemes cover:

- fire doors and shutters;
- fire alarm control and indicating equipment;
- call point systems, detectors and call points;
- sprinkler and water spray systems;
- halon and carbon dioxide systems;
- structural fire protection materials and systems;
- central stations for fire and security alarms;
- intruder alarm systems.

Equipment receiving approval from the LPCB can use the LPCB mark and is featured in an annually published LPCB list of approved products and services.

Fire Protection Association

The role of the FPA is primarily educational, but it also provides technical and general advice in all aspects of fire protection for industry, commerce and the general public. It analyses reports on all the major fires that occur and publishes the results in its journal, ten times a year.

As the national fire safety organisation, it makes up-to-date information on fire hazards, new materials and processes and equipment to prevent or contain fires available to the public.

Loss Prevention Council Technical Centre

The centre is concerned with testing and developing structural fire protection, fire protection equipment, security equipment, workplace loss prevention and environmental health and safety. It makes its testing facilities available to manufacturers with testing done in the strictest confidence and undertakes consultancy work reviewing fire safety in companies.

Facilities include:

- furnaces;
- test equipment;
- laboratories;
- ability to handle large-scale simulations.

National Approval Council for Security Systems

The objective of NACOSS is to raise standards amongst companies that install all types of security systems.

Any company that wants approval must undergo rigorous testing by NACOSS inspectors, to ensure that the company meets the necessary standards of:

- technical operation;
- maintenance of completed installations;
- staff conduct and training;

and that it follows codes of practice for customer relations and documentation control. NACOSS is also keen to reduce the numbers of false alarms.

A 'List of Approved Firms' is published annually by NACOSS, and approved firms are inspected regularly to ensure that they continue to meet the British standards.

NACOSS produces codes of practice on:

- security screening of personnel;
- customer communications;

- management of subcontracting;
- compilation of company control manuals;
- customer complaints;
- false alarms;
- intruder alarms;
- closed-circuit television;
- access control.

Marine and aviation insurance

Introduction

Both marine and aviation are specialist covers that require careful placing and are therefore beyond the scope of this guide.

You are advised to consult specialist publications for in-depth information on these subjects.

Marine insurance

There are four main areas of risk in marine insurance:

* *hull* – loss of, or damage to, the actual structure of the ship itself (cover provided under Institute Time Clauses (Hulls) 1/10/83);
* *cargo* – loss of, or damage to, cargo carried or in the process of being loaded (cover provided under Institute Cargo Clauses (A), (B), (C) 1/1/82);
* *freight* – loss of the fees paid for the carriage of cargo (cover provided under Institute Time Clauses – Freight 1/8/89, or Institute Voyage Clauses – Freight 1/8/89;
* *liabilities* – part insured under hull policies, part by protecting and indemnity clubs.

Periods of cover

Cover can be effected for different time periods:

* voyage policy: provides cover for the duration of a voyage;
* time policy: specifies the period of cover;
* mixed policy: cover for voyage and a specified time thereafter;
* construction policy: cover during construction, trials and until delivery;
* floating policy: cover for agreed sum large enough to cover a number of shipments;

- open cover: cover arranged in general terms, which applies to all shipments within its provisions, subject to adequate declaration of details of each cargo despatch.

Aviation insurance

Hull and liability are the main risks in aviation insurance, both of which are insured on the standard policy AVN 1A, in three sections covering:

- loss of, or damage to aircraft;
- legal liabilities to third parties who are not passengers;
- legal liabilities to passengers.

Additional clauses can be used to extend policy cover.

The liabilities of air carriers are governed by two agreements:

- The Warsaw Convention 1929: subject to monetary limits compensation must be paid to passengers without the carrier's negligence having to be proven.
- The Hague Protocol 1955: raised some of the limits in the Warsaw Convention.

These agreements have generally been adopted worldwide, whereas later agreements have not been ratified by all countries.

Market associations

Below is a list of insurance market associations.

Association of British Insurers (ABI)

See separate section.

Association of Insurance and Risk Managers in Industry and Commerce (AIRMIC)

Membership of over 500 buyers of insurance for large industrial or commercial companies or public services.

British Insurance and Investment Brokers Association (BIIBA)

National body that represents brokers engaged in general and investment business. Its objective is to represent its members' interests in much the same way as the ABI does for insurance companies. There is no requirement for brokers to belong to the BIIBA.

Chartered Insurance Institute (CII)

Professional body with educational objectives, membership exceeds 30,000 worldwide. Offers extensive educational and examination programme. Members must abide by the Code of Conduct, which requires them to behave with professionalism at all times.

Institute of Insurance Brokers (IIB)

Alternative organisation to BIIBA above.

Investment Managers' Regulatory Organisation (IMRO)

This organisation regulates the activities of investment and unit trust managers, investment trust managers, pension fund managers, trustees and firms advising commercial institutions on investments, following the requirements of the Financial Services Act 1986. Membership includes most of the UK large banks.

Institute of Risk Management (IRM)

Provides professional qualifications in risk management.

Personal Investment Authority (PIA)

Set up under the Financial Services Act 1986 to regulate the activities of independent financial advisers and product providers. The PIA became effective in 1994, taking over the roles of the previous regulatory organisations FIMBRA (Financial Intermediaries, Managers and Broker Regulatory Association) and LAUTRO (Life Assurance and Unit Trust Regulatory Organisation).

Securities and Futures Association (SFA)

The self-regulatory organisation for stockbrokers, securities dealers, market makers and futures and options brokers and dealers which ensures that the requirements of the Financial Services Act 1986 are met.

Medical expenses insurance

Introduction

Also known as private medical insurance or private health insurance, this form of cover gives individuals access to private medical treatment outside the National Health Service. They can thus have their choice of hospital, specialists or consultants, and decide on the timing for their treatment.

This form of cover is often arranged on a group basis, with cover being provided for all of an insured's employees.

Policy cover

Indemnity is provided against the costs of private medical treatment needed as a result of unforeseen illness or injury. The insured and eligible dependants are usually included in policy cover.

Benefits are paid in respect of hospital and nursing home accommodation, specialists' and consultants' fees and paramedical services such as physiotherapy and home nursing.

A limit is normally set on the total benefit that can be claimed in any one year, or a maximum level for specialists' fees or accommodation charges.

Different levels of cover are available to coincide with the insured's needs. If the National Health Service is used, a cash benefit is normally payable.

Low-cost restricted cover schemes offer policy benefits only if NHS treatment is unavailable for more than a certain number of weeks.

Policies exclude pre-existing conditions and do not include treatment outside Great Britain.

Risk assessment

The proposer's medical history will be subject to detailed underwriting consideration, and additional information will be sought from the proposer's doctor if necessary.

185

Group schemes

Substantial discounts are available for group schemes because of the administrative savings and probable improvement in results for the insurer. A group can be formed in a number of ways, which are treated slightly differently.

Affinity groups

These are made up of individuals who are connected by a set of common circumstances, e.g. members of a sports club, and attract premium discounts of 10% to 15%.

Employee schemes

The costs of the scheme and those people to be part of the scheme are the responsibility of employees, whose employer merely agrees to facilitate the scheme by collecting premiums and marketing its availability. Employee schemes attract a discount of 25%. The group must exceed a specified minimum number and each applicant must provide full details of their medical history.

Assisted schemes

Employer and employee share the costs of such schemes, which attract similar discounts.

Company paid schemes

The entire cost of the scheme is borne by the employer, who must appoint a 'group secretary' to look after the scheme records and the distribution of any other documentation such as marketing literature.

Different considerations apply to different sized groups:

Small groups

These have between three and 100 employees (and their dependants if the scheme allows), each of whom must provide a full medical history, failing which the policy will exclude illnesses which already exist when the cover is effected.

Large groups

These have over 100 employees and as the group is larger, the premium is lower for each applicant. There is usually no need for medical histories to be provided and normal underwriting requirements are waived. The average number of scheme members is declared at the end of the period of insurance and premiums are adjusted in line with this.

If the group is sufficiently large, subsequent rates may be based on its individual claims experience, rather than on statistical averages.

Money insurance

Introduction

Money insurance provides cover for situations where money is stolen or lost outside the normal theft definition involving forcible and violent entry into or exit from premises.

Policy cover

The policy covers both negotiable and non-negotiable money, but different limits apply. Negotiable money is that which the thief could spend or convert into its face value very easily; non-negotiable money needs to be passed through a bank and is therefore much less attractive to thieves.

The insured chooses a limit for the amount of negotiable money to be covered, which defines the insurer's maximum liability. A limit is also set by the insured for money in safes.

Other forms of money are subject to policy limits set by insurers:

- non-negotiable money: limit of £250,000;
- money kept on the insured's premises when they are closed, but not in a safe: limit up to £200;
- money in homes of company's directors or employees: limit up to £300 (if this is a regular event and a safe has been installed, a limit of up to £500 may apply);
- loss of or damage to safes: limit of indemnity is the repair or replacement cost;
- loss of or damage to clothing and personal effects through theft or attempted theft: limit of £500.

Cover applies for all risks, within the overall territorial limits, but in four specific locations:

- on the insured's premises during the insured's normal business hours;
- in transit;
- in the night safe of a bank until removed by a representative of the bank;

- in the home of a director or employee of the company or anyone else to whom it has been entrusted.

Exclusions

The policy will exclude losses arising from:

- employees' fraud or dishonesty;
- book-keeping errors;
- safes or strongrooms opened by keys or lock combinations left on premises.

Conditions

Those conditions that apply to most general property insurance policies will apply to the money insurance policy:

- policy voidable at insurer's option at renewal;
- insured required to notify insurer of any changes in the risk;
- insured must take reasonable precautions to ensure that losses do not occur;
- notification of claims;
- insurer's rights following a claim;
- contribution and subrogation;
- arbitration;
- any other insurance (in this instance fidelity guarantee).

In addition, the policy will include a condition requiring the insured to provide a declaration of actual figures for turnover and numbers of employees at the end of the period of insurance so that the estimates on which the policy rating has been based can be adjusted.

Extensions

It is possible for the insured to extend the policy by endorsement to include:

- cover for personal accident benefits for employees assaulted in a robbery or attempted robbery;
- contingency cover only, if a security firm is actually handling the insured's money operations;
- losses arising from the fraudulent use of credit cards (subject to a limit per card).

Rating factors

The main factor is the location of the risk, with big cities posing higher risks. The underwriter would then want to know what the annual carryings (exposure to cash handling and cash in transit) are estimated to be for the period to be insured and would apply a rate per mille (‰) to the figure. Also of relevance would be the limit set for money in locked safes during business hours, which would be subject to a rate per cent.

The premium based on estimated figures would be adjusted at the end of the insurance term once the insured declared what the actual figures had been.

A premium load will be made for personal accident cover, either of a fixed sum or a percentage of total premium.

Premium reductions are available for the use of professional security firms.

Checklist: Risk assessment

Insurers will consider the following to be material in assessing a money insurance risk:

- how often journeys transporting money are made;
- transport and protection;
- distance money has to be carried;
- number of people involved in each journey;
- estimated annual total value of money paid into and withdrawn from a bank, collected and transported;
- applicable limits for money in transit and on premises in business hours, in locked safe/strongroom outside business hours and stamped National Insurance cards;
- security protection for safe and strongroom keys outside business hours;
- safe or strongroom details.

For very high risk premises insurers may insist on specialist security protection.

Warranties

To insist that the insured complies with the insurer's requirements some of these are likely to be incorporated in the policy as warranties, so that if the insured does breach them, the policy will become void.

Examples would be the exclusion of losses through access to safe keys, and the installation of approved security alarms in designated high-risk areas.

Motor insurance

Introduction

The Road Traffic Acts make either motor insurance, or the lodging of a deposit of £250,000 with the Supreme Court, compulsory for anyone using a motor vehicle on a public highway.

As there are so many similarities between the main classes of motor insurance (private and commercial motor and motor cycle insurance), it is helpful to look at them together.

Private motor insurance

Private motor insurance provides the best basis for an understanding of the other forms of motor insurance.

Compulsory requirements

Any motor insurance policy must provide the insured with cover:

- against any liability that, through the use of a motor vehicle on a road in Great Britain, they may incur in respect of the death of, or bodily injury or damage to the property of any person;
- whilst the vehicle is used in GB if it is usually based elsewhere in the EU;
- whilst the vehicle is being used in any part of the EU other than GB if it is usually based in GB;
- in respect of their liability (under the RTA 88) to pay for emergency treatment.

The Road Traffic Act 1988 is the latest piece of road traffic legislation relating to compulsory motor insurance. The intention of successive pieces of legislation has been to ensure that funds are available to meet any liabilities incurred through the use of a motor vehicle on a road in Great Britain. It therefore requires anyone who will use a vehicle to take out insurance or obtain a security in respect of their third party liabilities.

The minimum cover that can legally be provided by a policy issued under the RTA 88 is:

- unlimited liability for bodily injury or death to third parties including passengers;
- up to £250,000 cover for damage to property belonging to third parties (to comply with the Second EC Motor Insurance Directive 1988);
- indemnity for claimants' and claim handling costs;
- cover for emergency medical treatment fees and hospital charges arising from the use of the vehicle.

Since the Third EC Motor Insurance Directive 1992, all motor insurance policies issued in the EC must provide:

- the minimum cover for any other EU country being visited (or cover for the country where the vehicle is normally kept, whichever is the higher);
- liability to persons employed by the insured when travelling in the course of their employment (this was previously covered in the UK by employer's liability policies).

This minimum cover was known as RTA cover, but since the inclusion of third party property damage as a minimum, the distinction between RTA cover and third party only cover has almost disappeared and RTA cover is extremely rare, with third party only being the minimum level of cover generally available.

Cover available

Third party only	Third party fire and theft	Comprehensive
• unlimited indemnity for death, bodily injury or property damage • claimants' costs and claims handling costs • emergency medical	Third party only cover, PLUS the cost of repairs if the vehicle is: • damaged by fire, lightning or explosion • damaged whilst stolen or during an attempt to	Third party fire and theft cover, PLUS cover for: • accidental or malicious damage to the insured's car and recovery and redelivery costs • personal accident

Third party only	Third party fire and theft	Comprehensive
treatment and hospital charges • minimum cover in other EU countries • employer's liability risk for insured's employees when travelling in the course of their employment • indemnity for accidents while the insured is driving a car or motor cycle which he or she does not own • indemnity to anyone driving or using the vehicle on the insured's order or with their permission • indemnity to the insured's passengers, employers or partners if held responsible for an accident • legal costs to defend a claim	steal it • stolen and not recovered	benefits on a given scale, such as: (a) death £5,000 (b) total loss of, or loss of sight in eye(s) £5,000 (c) total loss of, or loss of use of, limb(s) £5,000 • medical expenses (for a nominal amount) for the insured or passenger • rugs, clothing and personal effects, up to £100 if lost or damaged through theft, attempted theft or accident • up to 35 days whilst vehicle is being used in another part of the EU or in Austria, Czech Republic, Slovakia, Finland, Hungary, Norway or Switzerland

Third party only	Third party fire and theft	Comprehensive
• costs of up to £1,000 to defend a prosecution for manslaughter or death by dangerous or reckless driving		• reduction of premium if no claims during periods of insurance: no claims discount clause • car sharing agreements, if only the running costs of the vehicle are covered; the vehicle is not adapted to carry more than eight passengers and fares are agreed before the journey begins

The comprehensive policy excludes:

- wear, tear and depreciation;
- loss of use;
- mechanical or electrical failure or breakdown;
- bursts or punctured tyres.

An excess will also apply if the vehicle is being used or driven by a young and/or inexperienced driver when an incident giving rise to a claim occurs.

Checklist: Optional policy extensions

Windscreens

Such cover is usually included in a comprehensive policy and may be added to a non-comprehensive policy, subject to an additional premium.

Caravans and trailers

Whilst attached to the insured vehicle, these are usually covered for third party risks.

Racing, competitions, rallies and trials

Events such as road safety rallies may be covered at limited additional charge, whilst only a few specialist insurers offer cover for racing.

Rugs, clothing and personal effects

Included in a comprehensive policy, but only for a fairly limited sum. Optional extension grants increased monetary cover in return for an additional premium.

Young drivers

A truly occasional young additional driver may be included, subject to an additional premium.

Personal accident benefits

Provides additional personal accident benefits to those provided as standard in the comprehensive policy, e.g. increased capital benefits or weekly benefits for insured or spouse.

Car sharing agreements

Private motor policies exclude carriage for hire and reward. If a passenger does not pay more than the running costs of the vehicle; if the vehicle is not adapted to carry more than eight passengers and if fares are agreed before the journey begins, such fares do not constitute the vehicle being used for hire and reward.

Elections

Motor vehicles are sometimes used in connection with elections, which is not usually regarded as social, domestic or pleasure use. Additional premium is not usually charged for the removal of this exception, unless use is for a parliamentary election.

Accidents to paid drivers

Cover is available for the legal liabilities of the insured in respect of accidents to paid drivers during the course of their employment. Cover applies only to domestic servants – other employees must be covered by a specific employer's liability policy.

Breakdown cover

Some policies allow the insured to telephone a control centre for assistance in the event of a breakdown, and for an additional premium, cover the cost of the call-out charge, an hour's labour for roadside repair and towing the car to a garage.

Joint policies

Policies may be issued in joint names, such as those of a policyholder and spouse. Additional premium depends on the cover required.

Loss of use

Some insurers offer loss of use cover, limited to an amount per day and subject to an additional premium. A few will pay for a replacement vehicle for a limited period while the insured's vehicle is off the road.

Exclusions

These apply to all sections of the policy.

Description of vehicle

Where a blanket certificate is issued the insurer must be notified of any change of vehicle within seven days and any liability under the policy is excluded if this requirement is not met.

Use of insured vehicle

Insurers will not be liable:

- if the vehicle is being used other than as specified in the certificate of motor insurance;
- if the policyholder does not hold a licence or is disqualified; or
- if the car is driven by a person not specified in the policy whom the policyholder knows does not have a licence.

Contractual liability

The insurer cannot become liable under the policy through the operation of a contract where otherwise no liability would have existed.

The other exclusions are standard to all motor insurance policies:

- war risks;
- radioactive contamination;
- riot and civil commotion;
- sonic bangs.

Commercial motor insurance

A standard policy is commonly used for all commercial insurances and modified as necessary to fit a particular risk.

Commercial vehicles can be split into groups:

- goods-carrying vehicles;
- passenger-carrying vehicles;
- agricultural and forestry vehicles;
- special types such as cranes, hearses and road rollers.

Policy cover

The policy provides:

- unlimited indemnity for death or bodily injury of third parties;
- property damage up to a maximum of £1 million, but this limit can be increased;
- cover for interruption of traffic flow following a contents spill, up to a limit of £1 million;
- liabilities incurred during loading or unloading;
- indemnity to anyone driving the vehicle with the insured's permission;
- indemnity to anyone using the vehicle for social, domestic or pleasure purposes;
- indemnity to passengers;
- legal costs for representation at a coroner's inquest, fatal inquiry or a Court of Summary Jurisdiction;
- other costs incurred with the insurer's consent;
- costs of defence against a charge of manslaughter or causing death by dangerous or reckless driving;
- indemnity to any principal with whom the insured has an agreement;
- indemnity to any hirer of the vehicle;
- indemnity to the insured's legal personal representatives;
- contingency cover for employees' vehicles being used on the policyholder's business;
- cover in the rest of the EU to the minimum legal requirement;

- third party cover for trailers whilst attached to the insured vehicle;
- third party risk for broken-down vehicles while being towed.

Exceptions to third party section

The policy will not provide cover for losses arising:

- from loading other than by driver or attendant beyond limits of carriageway;
- from employer's liability risks;
- from persons without driving licences;
- if the person claiming indemnity gave permission to drive to a person known not to have a licence;
- if indemnified by another policy;
- to the policyholder's property.

The policy types available are the same as for the private motor insurance policy, third party only, third party fire and theft and comprehensive. There are minor differences between the private and commercial comprehensive policies:

- cover for accidental damage only applies to spare parts and accessories whilst they are attached to the vehicle;
- cover can be applied to trailers and vehicles being towed, whilst attached;
- cover can be applied for broken-down vehicles whilst attached for towing;
- the policy does not include cover for driving other cars not owned by the insured;
- personal accident benefits, personal effects and medical expenses are not covered.

Checklist: Optional extensions to the commercial vehicle policy

The policy can be extended on payment of an additional premium, to include:

- an increased third party property damage limit, or the limit can be removed completely;
- medical expenses and personal accident benefits;
- rugs, clothing and personal effects cover;
- windscreen cover or the limit can be increased;

- the insured's indemnity for loss, damage or liability arising from his or his employees' negligence while the vehicle is in a hirer's custody or control;
- cover for the hirer for loss, damage or liability from his own or his employees' negligence;
- indemnity to principal, if the vehicle is used in connection with contract work;
- carnivals;
- cover for sheets and ropes if these are in a locked place in the vehicle;
- loss of use – up to 80% of the cost of hiring a replacement vehicle following accidental damage, fire or theft in the UK or Western Europe.

Conditions

These are the same as for the private car policy, plus:

- application of limits of indemnity – the policyholder's liabilities will be met under the policy before those of other persons liable, so that if the limit of indemnity is reached, the policyholder will have been indemnified;
- limit of indemnity exceeded – if a claim is likely to exceed the limit set, the insurer has the right to pay the amount of the limit to the insured and leave him to settle the claim himself.

Exclusions

The same general exclusions apply as to the private motor policy, plus:

- the use of the vehicle other than as specified in the policy schedule is excluded;
- racing, pace-making, reliability, trials and speed testing.

Risk assessment

For both private and commercial motor policies, proposal forms are used to elicit information under the following headings:

- proposer;
- car;
- cover;
- drivers;
- use;

- no claim discount (NCD).

Use is an important consideration, with most insurers offering three or four classes:

- use for social, domestic and pleasure purposes only;
- use by the policyholder and/or spouse in person in connection with his or her business (business use limited to insured and spouse);
- use in connection with the business or profession of the policyholder (any driver covered by the policy can drive the vehicle of the insured's business);
- commercial travelling (the vehicle can be used for commercial travelling).

Use for hire and reward and in connection with the motor trade would be excluded from all classes.

For the commercial vehicle proposal, additional questions are asked on:

- the business (a description will be sought);
- the vehicle and its carrying capacity;
- use. The classes for commercial vehicles are: carriage of own goods, carriage of own goods plus those of others for hire and reward within a set radius of insured's depot, haulage contractor.

Both proposals include a declaration to be accompanied by the proposer's signature, to confirm that the answers given are correct to the best of the proposer's knowledge and belief.

Rehabilitation of Offenders Act 1974

This Act enables certain offenders who are not re-convicted, after a period of time, to become rehabilitated persons and to act as if they had not been convicted. 'Spent' convictions need not therefore be disclosed after a minimum period of five years.

Endorsements for RTA offences may be removed after four years, except for offences relating to driving or attempting to drive under the influence of alcohol or drugs, in which case the relevant rehabilitation period is 11 years:

- such convictions need not be disclosed;
- insurers cannot include questions to seek information on such convictions;
- if information is disclosed, insurers cannot use it to set a rate.

Checklist: Rating motor insurance

The underwriter determines the correct premium for each risk by considering these factors:

Private motor

The vehicle:

- type of vehicle;
- age/value of vehicle;
- use of vehicle;
- area of use;
- type of cover.

The driver:

- age;
- occupation;
- experience;
- disabilities;
- insurance history;
- motoring convictions.

Commercial motor

Goods-carrying vehicles:

- type of vehicle;
- use;
- district;
- policy cover;
- driver.

Hire cars:

- type of use: private, public or self-drive hire;
- district;
- cover;
- drivers;
- maintenance of vehicle.

Passenger-carrying vehicles:

- number of passengers carried;
- district of use;

- value;
- drivers.

Agricultural vehicles – flat rates usually apply based on value:

- cover;
- type of vehicle;
- purpose of use;
- district of use.

Vehicles of special construction – flat rates usually apply based on value:

- plant-type, e.g. bulldozers;
- special-type, e.g. hearses.

General policy conditions

These apply to both private and commercial motor policies:

Duties of policyholder

- the policyholder must observe the terms of the policy; and
- answer the questions on the proposal form honestly and to the best of their knowledge and belief.

Notification

- the insured must notify accidents, claims or civil proceedings to insurers in writing as soon as possible; and
- send any letters or writs to the insurer immediately.

Control of claims/subrogation

- the insured must make no admission of liability without the insurer's consent;
- insurers are entitled to pursue the insured's rights against any third party;
- the conduct of proceedings or settlement of the claim is at the insurer's discretion.

Cancellation

The policy may be cancelled:

- by the insurer: by seven days' notice by letter to the policyholder's last known address. Return of premium is then due to policyholder;

- by the policyholder: then will be entitled to premium return at short period rates, calculated once certificate has been returned.

Contribution

Insurers are liable to pay only their rateable proportion of any claim that is also covered by another insurance policy covering the same risk and perils.

Maintenance and condition of vehicle

The insured must maintain the vehicle in roadworthy condition, safeguard it from loss or damage and permit the insurer access to examine it at all times.

Arbitration

Disputes about the amount to be paid in settlement of a claim will be referred to an independent arbitrator.

Monthly premiums

If a due monthly premium is not paid, the insurer is not liable from the date of the missed payment, but will send a letter giving seven days' notice of cancellation to the policyholder before ceasing to provide cover.

Fleets

If an insured has a large number of vehicles, they constitute a fleet. A small fleet may comprise between 10 and 30 vehicles, while a large fleet would contain over 100 vehicles.

Rating

Small fleets: individual rates are calculated for each vehicle with a discount from total premium for the fact that a fleet is being covered.

Medium fleets: results can be spoiled by single large losses and the insurer will select a way of assessing the overall performance and discounting the effect of the few large losses.

Large fleets: the past three years' claims figures are adjusted to negate the impact of inflation. Claims figures are divided by the number of vehicle years for the same period (insurance of one vehicle for one year) to give the 'burning cost' – the actual cost of likely future claims. This figure has to be adjusted for inflation, expenses and an element of profit before a premium can be determined.

Fleet surveys

Insurers may offer a risk assessment survey of a fleet to look at claims patterns and suggest ways in which the fleet owner could eliminate, minimise or transfer risk.

Motor cycle insurance

Policies must insure the same liabilities as private motor policies, and similar types of cover are available under third party only, third party fire and theft and comprehensive policies.

The comprehensive policy differs from the private motor comprehensive policy in that:

- spare parts and accessories are not covered for theft unless the bike is also stolen at the same time;
- the liability section only indemnifies the insured and his legal personal representatives in the event of his death, not other third parties;
- no personal accident benefits, medical expenses cover or personal effects cover is included;
- a compulsory excess applies for fire, theft or accidental damage claims.

Extensions

For payment of an additional premium, cover can be provided for:

- trailers;
- driving other cycles (if otherwise excluded);
- more than one cycle insured at same time (with possible premium reduction);
- invalid carriages.

Types of policy

Motor cycle insurance can either be written on a specified motor cycle or on a specified rider basis.

Specified motor cycle cover allows the driver to drive one particular bike only.

Specified rider cover allows the driver to drive any motor cycle, as the driver and not the cycle is the subject-matter of insurance.

Rating

Rating factors include:

- driver's age;
- occupation;
- cubic capacity (engine size) of cycle;
- where cycle is garaged;
- type of cover required.

Conditions

The standard conditions and exclusions apply, as for the private motor policy.

Motor Insurers' Bureau (MIB)

Introduction

The MIB was formed in 1945. It operates the green card system and provides compensation for people injured in motor accidents if compensation isn't available from any other source. Membership of the MIB is compulsory for all UK motor insurers and is a condition of their authorisation. It is funded by its members, through periodic contributions in line with the member's premium income.

Green cards

The International Insurance Certificate is commonly known as a green card (through being printed on green paper). Prior to the First EC Motor Insurance Directive, a green card was needed by any motorist wishing to take their motor vehicle out of the UK, to demonstrate that insurance was in force to meet the legal requirements of the countries being visited.

The UK motorist's own certificate of insurance is now proof of this for EU countries, as any motor insurance policies issued in an EU country must meet the minimum legal requirements of all other EU member states.

Green cards are still issued to insureds as the proof of insurance most easily recognised through Western Europe.

New agreements

Concern was expressed that the numbers of accidents caused by drivers who had no insurance or who were untraced were defeating the purpose of motor insurance being made compulsory, i.e. to make funds available to compensate those who were injured or whose property was damaged as a result of a road traffic accident. In response to this, the MIB entered into two new agreements with its member companies.

Uninsured drivers agreement

In most cases, the uninsured motorist will have a policy that is invalid for some reason, or which has recently expired. In such cases the Road Traffic Act insurer, i.e. the one to have issued the policy, will deal with the matter on behalf of the MIB.

A victim of an uninsured motorist who obtains a judgement against the motorist, can call on the MIB to satisfy the judgement if the wrongdoer does not pay the necessary amount within seven days. Alternatively, with the motorist's agreement, the MIB will settle the claim out of court. In either case the offending motorist will be liable to reimburse the MIB for the amount of the judgement.

Following the First EC directive and the 1988 Road Traffic Act, the MIB also became liable to settle, or ensure settlement of, property damage claims up to a maximum of £250,000 per accident, if caused by an uninsured driver. It is not responsible for property damage caused by an untraced driver. The MIB is not responsible for the first £175 of any property damage claim, to avoid the need for its involvement in small claims.

Untraced drivers agreement

This applies to hit-and-run accidents where the driver cannot be traced. The MIB undertakes to provide compensation if it can be established that on the balance of probabilities the untraced motorist would be liable to pay damages to the accident victim or their heirs. The MIB selects a member company on a rota basis to deal with such claims.

No claim discounts

Scales

Most insurers operating NCD schemes publish a scale of discounts for claim-free years. A typical example is given below:

Claim-free years	No claim discount
One	30%
Two	40%
Three	50%
Four	60%
Five and more	65%

Claims

Originally, making a claim would have meant that the policyholder lost all the discount and had to start again. This practice has been superseded by the 'step back' practice, which reduces the number of years during which no claims have been made. It is usual to knock two years off for each claim. The discount then applies at a lower level.

Case study

If someone has maximum NCD of five years (which could represent any higher number of years without claim) and is involved in an accident resulting in a claim being made on the policy, the policy will be stepped back by two years to three years' entitlement and a discount of 50% rather than 65% will apply to the next year's premium. It will take the policyholder another two years to return his or her entitlement to the maximum level.

Renewals

A policyholder can claim on the policy and still retain NCD if the claim is settled in his or her favour and the insurer recovers all of its outlay. If a claim of this sort is still under negotiation when renewal is invited, it will be invited at the higher figure, as if NCD has been lost. If the policy is renewed and the claim settled without cost to the insurer, then a refund will be given to the policyholder when the NCD is subsequently reinstated.

Protected NCD

In view of the reluctance of policyholders to lose discount entitlement once gained, a further development was the introduction of no claim discount protection.

This gives a policyholder with maximum entitlement to NCD the opportunity to pay a slightly higher premium in return for the ability to make up to two claims in a specified period (commonly five years) without no claims discount being reduced.

Transferring NCD

If policyholders wish to move from one insurer to another, they can usually retain their discount entitlement, so long as their original insurers confirm the amount of their entitlement to their new insurers.

Pensions

Introduction

This is an extremely complex subject and beyond the scope of this guide. It is always essential to obtain professional advice in any matter relating to the provision of pensions.

A brief outline of the main types of pension available is given below.

State pension

For those without any form of private pension provision, there are two parts to the state pension: the basic state pension and the State Earnings Related Pension (SERPS). Benefits from these pensions alone are unlikely to provide a comfortable level of income in retirement.

Occupational pensions

Employers have no legal obligation to provide pension schemes, but many do so. Such schemes can be contributory, where members pay a specified contribution, normally a percentage of salary, or non-contributory where the employer makes all the contributions.

Schemes can be run privately, sometimes with the help of professional advisers; or can be delegated to an insurance company. The scheme will specify the normal retirement date (NRD) for members, which can be any age between 60 and 75 for both sexes.

Schemes provide:

- benefits on retirement: the maximum payable is two-thirds final salary for the rest of the member's life, taxed as earned income. Part of the pension can be taken as a lump sum subject to Inland Revenue limits and will not be taxed;
- benefits on death after retirement: i.e. pension for widow/er or other dependants up to a maximum of two-thirds of the member's pension provided at retirement;
- benefits on death in service: i.e. either a pension for the widow/er,

which usually ceases on death or remarriage, or a lump sum payment up to a maximum of four times the member's salary at the date of death.

Additional Voluntary Contributions (AVCs) can be paid by qualifying members as long as total benefits remain within Inland Revenue limits.

Schemes can contract-in to SERPS or contract-out, in which case no SERPS benefit will be paid in respect of the relevant period of service. Any scheme contracting-out must provide at least the same level of benefit as SERPS.

An employee leaving service before normal retirement date can receive:

- a refund of their own contributions (subject to tax) if they have less than two years' service;
- a deferred payment;
- a transfer payment to buy into another scheme or a personal pension.

Personal pensions

These can be provided by a variety of institutions including banks, building societies and insurance companies, most of which offer a similar range of investment funds and life products and are the only option for pension provision for self-employed people.

Employed people may choose a personal pension because:

- their employer does not provide a pension scheme; or
- they are not eligible for their employer's scheme; or
- they choose not to join their employer's scheme.

Personal pensions are always provided on a 'defined contribution' (money-purchase scheme) basis. An employer can contribute to an employee's personal pension. Contributions are limited to a specific percentage of earnings dependent upon age.

Personal pensions cannot be surrendered for cash or assigned before retirement, but can provide almost the same types of benefits as group pension schemes. The Inland Revenue limits contributions, rather than benefits payable.

Common benefits:

- pension on retirement at age from 50 to 75: there is no limit to the pension that can be payable, which will be whatever can be bought by the accumulated pension fund. An annuity can be bought to provide the pension;
- lump sum on retirement: this must be paid when the annuity starts. Up to 25% of the total fund can be taken as a tax-free lump sum, the rest

must be used to buy pension benefits;
- lump sum on death before retirement: the fund bought with the contributions to the date of death is normally returned;
- widow/er's pension.

The pension holder has a choice of the benefits and features that they want to be included in the contract. Waiver of premium benefit may be included.

Benefits can be transferred between different personal pension schemes and to and from occupational schemes; any transfer payments must represent the cash equivalent of the individual's assumed rights to benefits under the scheme.

A personal pension receives the following tax concessions:

- tax relief on contributions;
- contributions invested in a tax-free fund;
- tax-free lump sum at retirement;
- contributions made by employers are exempt benefits-in-kind and therefore employees are not taxed on them.

Pension payments are taxed as earned income.

Annuity

At retirement, the accumulated pension fund is usually used to buy an annuity, to provide the insured (the annuitant) with an income for the rest of his or her life. Annuities are provided by insurance companies and the rates will differ in line with prevailing economic conditions when they are bought.

The premium, a lump sum, is invested and the returns from that investment fund the income for the insured.

There are several different types of annuity:

- immediate annuity: payments will start as soon as the lump sum payment has been made;
- deferred annuity: payments will start at some future date;
- guaranteed annuity: if the insured dies within the guarantee period agreed upon, some proportion of the contributions towards the annuity will be returned to his or her estate;
- non-guaranteed annuity: no return of contributions will be made, regardless of how soon after the inception date of the annuity the insured person dies.

Annuities can be written to cover a single life, or two lives, or the survivor of two lives.

Permanent health insurance

Introduction

Permanent health insurance (PHI) is a long-term contract, which means that once cover has been granted, it cannot be withdrawn until the expiry date of the policy, usually timed to coincide with the policyholder's retirement.

Policy cover

The policy provides a regular payment to the insured if he or she becomes unable to work following an accident or illness. The payment will continue until either:

- the insured recovers;
- the insured retires;
- the insured dies; or
- the end of the policy term;

whichever happens first.

Claims must be met regardless of the numbers made during the period of insurance, as long as the insured meets all policy conditions and pays the necessary renewal premiums.

No benefit is usually paid out until the end of a deferred period, commonly 4, 13, 26 or 52 weeks after the event giving rise to the claim. The deferred period has a direct link to the premium payable for the cover: the longer the period, the lower the premium.

Checklist: Definitions of disability

The definition of disability chosen will also contribute to the level of the premium, with the narrowest form of cover resulting in the lowest premiums.

The widest definition used, and therefore the one that carries the greatest risk for the insurer, is: 'the insured is unable, due to sickness or accident, to follow his or her own occupation'.

This allows the insured to claim from the policy if there is other work that he could do, but he is unable to do the work that he is accustomed to doing.

A narrower definition would be: 'the insured is unable, due to sickness or accident, to follow his or her own occupation or any other for which they are suited by training and experience'.

This is perhaps the most common definition, but there is an even more restricted form of cover that uses the definition: 'the insured is unable, due to sickness or accident, to follow any occupation'.

Other policy features

Proportionate benefit

In order to encourage the insured to return to work as soon as possible, the policy can be written so that proportionate benefit is available, which means that rather than benefit payment ceasing completely as soon as the insured does work of any kind, a level of benefit will continue to be paid in proportion to the difference between the insured's current level of earnings and that enjoyed before the disability.

Change of occupation

The insurer reserves the right to cancel the policy if the insured changes jobs, as the circumstances of the risk may change dramatically at the same time. Any change of job must be notified to the insurer.

Increasability option

This allows for policy benefits to keep pace with inflation.

Waiver of premium benefit

This releases the insured from the need to continue to pay premiums to keep the policy going, whilst at the same time receiving benefit under the policy.

Limit on benefits

This is imposed to ensure that the insured does not improve his or her financial situation by claiming benefits, which are therefore usually set at three-quarters of the salary earned before disablement, minus any state invalidity benefit payable and benefits from any other PHI policies.

Foreign residence and travel

Insurers normally provide cover only while the insured is within the 'free limits' – usually the UK and the Republic of Ireland. The policy can be extended to include cover for other areas.

Exclusions

The policy excludes claims arising from:

- self-inflicted injury or disease;
- the insured being under the influence of non-prescribed alcohol or drugs;
- taking part in a criminal act;
- childbirth, pregnancy or complications of these;
- war risks;
- aviation other than as a fare-paying passenger;
- AIDS.

Rating

Careful consideration will be given to the insured's occupation as the most important rating factor; some occupations being dangerous and others specialised. Insurers use classes to distinguish occupations, with Class 1 representing the lowest risk (office work) and Class 4 the highest risk (deep-sea divers and bomb disposal work).

Other important factors will be the insured's age and medical history, to assess the likelihood of the insured succumbing to illness in the future.

Group PHI schemes

A group PHI scheme can be written under a master policy issued to an employer, so that benefits can be provided to employees following their disablement during service with the employer.

The scheme will have certain rules, such as:

- minimum and maximum ages for cover to apply;
- the amount of qualifying service needed before an employee can join the scheme;
- employees eligible to join the scheme.

The amount of cover to be provided could either be a flat benefit or could be varied by salary group or based on a percentage of salary.

In return for the payment of additional premiums, schemes may waive premiums in respect of members claiming benefits, arrange for benefit payments to increase in line with a chosen rate or the Retail Prices Index to mitigate inflation, or operate on a profit share basis with the insurer and the employer benefiting from good claims experience on the account.

It is a condition of the policy that any member joining the scheme must meet the underwriting requirements of the scheme and that the insurer has the right to decline to offer cover to a particular employee or impose special terms if it considers this course of action appropriate.

Rating

Two bases of rating are used:

- annual premiums: level premiums based on applicant ages when they enter the scheme;
- single premiums: premiums revised each year in line with the level of risk that each individual member brings to the pool.

Non-selection limit

If an employee has been actively at work for a specified period before applying to join the scheme, they can be accepted without needing to provide evidence of health. A limit applies to benefits provided in these circumstances, known as the non-selection limit or the free cover level. If a higher level of benefit is sought, then evidence of health may be required before it can be granted.

To qualify for a non-selection limit, schemes must:

- define the benefits available to employees;
- have 90% of eligible employees join the scheme at its outset;
- require all future employees to join;
- permit the non-selection limit to be reviewed;
- limit scheme access to employees who have become eligible by completing two months actively at work prior to scheme entry;
- produce evidence of health for any member for whom benefits payable are to exceed the non-selection limit set.

Any claim payments under the scheme are usually made direct to the employer.

Personal accident and sickness insurance

Introduction

This form of insurance provides the insured with the security of knowing that in the event of an accident they or their dependants would receive a lump sum payment in compensation, and in the event of disability would receive a regular benefit for a period of time.

Policy cover

The cover provided under the accident section of the policy is for the payment of a lump sum in the event of the accidental death of the insured, or certain types of bodily injury to the insured, for example, the loss of a limb.

If an accident causes the insured to become disabled, either partially or totally, and either temporarily or permanently, a benefit payment is made to the insured.

The sickness section of the policy provides for similar benefits to be paid in the event of the disability of the insured as a result of sickness or disease. The definition of disablement makes reference to the insured no longer being able to follow his or her own occupation.

When a sickness benefit is to be paid, a franchise (see EXCESSES, DEDUCTIBLES, FRANCHISES) usually applies. This means that the insured can only claim if his or her illness exceeds a set number of days. However, if the illness does exceed the time franchise set, then benefit will be paid for the full period of sickness, including the franchise period. The franchise for this type of insurance is usually seven days, in order to discourage small claims.

Illness contracted within 21 days of the inception of the policy is usually excluded, as otherwise there may have been an element of selection against an insurer by an insured who suspected the onset of an illness.

Checklist: Policy benefits

Capital sums for accidents resulting in death or bodily injury, for example:

- death within 12 months of the event giving rise to the claim: £10,000;
- total loss of, or irrecoverable loss of, sight in one or both eyes: £10,000;
- total loss of one or both limbs within 12 or 24 months of the accident causing the injury: £10,000.

Capital sums or weekly benefits for events resulting in disablement, for example:

- permanent total disablement: payable once it is possible to be sure that disablement is both permanent and total, either a capital sum (e.g. £10,000) or an annuity providing smaller capital sums for a period of time (e.g. £1,000 for ten years);
- permanent partial disablement: a lesser capital sum is payable;
- temporary total disablement: a weekly benefit is payable for a maximum of 104 weeks (e.g. £100) if the insured is unable to engage in his or her usual occupation as a result of either accident or sickness;
- temporary partial disablement: if the insured is unable to engage in his or her usual occupation as a result of accident only, a weekly benefit is payable (e.g. £50).

A nominal amount of cover is also provided for medical expenses incurred for treatment following an accident.

Some policies can be extended to provide a limited amount of LEGAL EXPENSES INSURANCE, to enable the insured to meet the costs of pursuing an action against a third party responsible for the accident.

Exclusions

The policy excludes claims arising from:

- self-inflicted injury or disease;
- the insured being under the influence of alcohol or drugs;
- pre-existing defects or infirmities;
- childbirth, pregnancy, venereal disease or AIDS;
- war risks;
- sickness within 21 days of policy inception;
- the insured's involvement in dangerous sports or pastimes such as diving, mountaineering or aviation.

Cover will also only apply within certain age limits meant to represent the period during which the insured could be assumed to be following an occupation – age 16 to 65 are common for accident cover and 16 to 55 for sickness cover.

Group schemes

There are no significant differences between individual and group schemes except that groups attract significant discounts. Medical underwriting requirements are likely to be waived if all eligible employees enter the scheme, thus removing the possibility of selection against the insurer.

Benefit payments from members of group schemes are likely to be related to earnings, with lump sums being a selected multiple of salary and benefit payments a percentage of salary.

Group schemes are available both to groups of employees and also to other affinity groups, such as social clubs.

Policy form and schedule

Introduction

Although the contract of insurance exists regardless of whether or not there is a policy document, the policy is evidence of the contract.

Most policies are now pre-printed and follow a broadly similar structure, while varying in style and length. Scheduled policies that adapt a common wording to the particular needs of the insured are now usual. Increasingly personal insurance policies are written in plain English, so that their contents are more comprehensible.

Policy contents

The heading

The heading includes the name of the insurer and its address.

Preamble

The preamble states that the proposal form is the basis of the contract and is incorporated in it. It also refers to the fact that the insured has agreed to pay, or has paid, the premium, and in return confirms that the insurer will provide the cover detailed in the policy, subject to its terms and conditions.

Signature

A signature of an official of the company is contained within the policy.

Operative clause

This is the most important section of the policy and sets out the cover that the insurer promises to provide.

Exclusions

It is just as important for a policy to detail what will not be covered as what will be covered and this is the role of the exclusions. Exclusions can be general, in which case they apply to all sections of the policy (e.g. war, riot and civil commotion) or particular and apply only to set sections of the policy.

Endorsements

The policy can be endorsed to alter the cover provided by the standard policy wording. Endorsements are printed in some policy wordings, with reference being made to those which apply.

Conditions

The conditions set out the behaviour required of the insured and insurer in certain circumstances and also the rights that the insurer has in respect of the policy.

Several conditions are common to all policies:

- the insured will comply with the terms of the policy;
- the insured must notify the insurer of any changes in the risk;
- the procedures to be followed in the event of a claim are specified;
- the effect of fraud on the policy is explained;
- the insured must do everything reasonably possible to minimise any loss;
- arbitration: disputes will be referred to independent arbitration;
- contribution: if other policies cover the same risk they will contribute to a claim in rateable proportion;
- subrogation: the insurer may take over any rights that the insured has against a third party in order to recover some of its outlay;
- cancellation: the insurer's right to cancel the policy;
- adjustment: the insured must declare actual figures to the insurer if the premium is based on estimates.

If conditions are specified in the policy they are 'express', but if assumed (e.g. that the subject-matter of insurance exists) then they are said to be 'implied'.

Conditions may also be classified as:

- precedent to the contract: these must be fulfilled before the contract can be created;
- subsequent to the contract: must be complied with once the contract is in force;
- precedent to liability: relate to claims and must be complied with for cover to operate (although the ABI Statements of Practice require insurers not to avoid claims if the breach of condition was unrelated to the claim in question).

Policy schedule

This personalises the cover for the individual insured. It provides details of the insured and the risk and any variations in cover that apply. Typical information contained in a policy schedule is:

- the insured's name and address;
- the nature of the business;
- the period of insurance;
- premiums;
- the sums insured or limits of liability;
- the policy number;
- reference to any special exclusions, conditions or aspects of cover.

Premiums

Introduction

One of the jobs of the underwriter is to determine the appropriate premium for the risk.

The premium is the contribution that the insured must make to the common fund into which all policyholders pay and from which all claims are paid. It is essential that the premium represents the amount of risk that the policyholder brings to the fund, as otherwise the fund will be depleted and less able to meet claims from other policyholders. This assessment of risk and calculation of premium is at the heart of the underwriting process.

Functions

The premium must enable the insurer to:

- meet expected claims;
- create a reserve for claims not settled at the end of the policy term and a contingency reserve for future liabilities;
- cover its operating expenses;
- make a profit.

Other considerations to be borne in mind by the underwriter in setting premium rates are inflation, interest and exchange rates and competition.

Calculation

In working out what the premium should be for a particular risk, the underwriter will need to have two figures in mind: the premium base and the premium rate.

Premium base

This is the figure that reflects the potential exposure represented by the risk. For property insurance, it is likely to be the sum insured: the value of the insured's financial interest in the property at risk.

In a class of business such as employer's liability, there is not a specific sum insured, as the financial interest at risk is the insured's potential liability to pay an as yet unspecified amount in compensation to an employee injured at work. Here the premium base is likely to be some other measure of exposure to risk, like the total wage bill for the people employed by the insured.

Premium rate

The premium rate is an amount applied to the premium base, which will produce the premium for the risk. In commercial insurances this is usually expressed as a rate per cent (per £100 of the premium base), or a rate per mille (per £1,000). There are different rating factors taken into consideration for each class of business, which together indicate to the underwriter the appropriate rate for the risk.

Case study

If the premium base (sum insured) on a factory building insured against fire and special perils is £100,000 and the insurer considers the correct premium rate to be 7.5 per cent (7.5%), then the premium for the risk would be £7,500.

If the premium base (total wage bill) for the employer's liability risk for the same factory is £60,000 and the insurer considers the correct premium rate to be 10 per mille (10‰), then the premium for the risk would be £600.

Flat premiums

In some types of insurance, more frequently personal lines business, a flat premium will be charged for risks of a particular sort. The different levels of hazard associated with different types of risk are assessed and a rating table is produced to give set rates for particular combinations of hazards.

Case study

The best example is private motor insurance. Assume that you are trying to find a rate for a young driver with a group 6 car, living in Suffolk. You would look up the page for drivers between the ages of, say, 21 and 24 years and then find the rates that applied to Suffolk. Then you would look for the rates applicable to group 6 cars, and for cars that are older than ten

---

years. Finally, you would look for the rate that determined the types of cover to be offered. This would be the flat rate premium for the risk. Any discounts would be taken off this figure. Similarly, if you felt that the risk was greater than normal, perhaps because the proposer had a medical condition such as diabetes, any premium loading would be added to this figure.

The traditional underwriting guides that used to contain all of this information have largely now been overtaken by sophisticated computerised quotation systems, which can fine-tune rates according to distinctions between risks as small as the difference between two postcodes in the same street.

Adjustable premiums

It is not always possible to know exactly what the premium base will be at the start of a policy term. Take employer's liability insurance as an example again – if the premium is to be based on the total wage bill for the year, that would not be known until the year had ended, although an estimate could be made at the beginning of the year.

In these circumstances, the premium rate would be applied to the premium base estimated by the insured at the beginning of the year and then adjusted at the end of the insurance year when the actual premium base was known. The insured would be obliged by the policy to make a declaration of the actual figure to the insurer.

Level premiums

In life assurance, the risk of death increases each year as the person's age increases. If premiums were to increase in line with the increased risk at renewal each year, then the policy would eventually become unaffordable.

In view of this, at the inception of the policy the proposer will be told what the premium for the risk will be and this figure will not change throughout the term of the policy, as long as premium payments continue to be made and the policy continues in force.

Insurance Premium Tax (IPT)

This has applied since 1 October 1994 to most general insurance policies, but not to long-term insurances or reinsurance contracts.

The tax is payable by the insured, as a component of the premium, but it is the insurer that is responsible for collecting it and accounting for it to Customs and Excise.

The rate of tax is announced as part of the Budget each year. When introduced, it was 2.5% of written premium and for the 1997/98 tax year was 4%. With effect from 1 August 1998, IPT at 17.5% applies to travel insurance policies.

Products liability insurance

Introduction

The common law position on buying goods was *caveat emptor* or 'let the buyer beware'. Over the past 30 years, consumer legislation has increased, in turn placing an increasingly strict liability on those who manufacture and/or retail products.

Sale of Goods Act 1979 (amended by the Sale and Supply of Goods Act 1994)

Section 14 imposes a requirement on manufacturers or retailers that the goods must be of satisfactory quality.

'Satisfactory' is what a reasonable person would regard as satisfactory, bearing in mind any description of the goods, the price and any other circumstances. Assessment of the quality of the goods may include: their fitness for purpose, appearance and finish, freedom from minor defects, and safety and durability.

If a buyer inspects the goods before purchase and should have been able to decide on their quality, then no further question about quality arises.

The definition of satisfactory quality should also relate to second-hand or shop-soiled goods.

The implied condition of satisfactory quality applies to sales in the course of a business. It does not apply if the seller draws the attention of the buyer to a defect in the goods prior to sale.

Unfair Contract Terms Act 1977

This Act limits the extent to which liability for breach of contract or for negligence can be avoided by the use of contract terms, so that liability for death or bodily injury cannot be restricted and liability for loss or damage can only be restricted if the restriction is reasonable.

Reasonableness is the main test of whether or not a contract term is fair.

Unfair Contract Terms in Consumer Contracts Regulations 1994

These apply to most consumer contracts and provide that an unfair term in a consumer contract is not binding on the consumer and that contracts must be expressed in plain and clear language.

Consumer Protection Act 1987

This was introduced to comply with the EC Directive on Liability for Defective Products (85/374/EEC).

It imposes a strict liability on the producer of a product where damage (death, personal injury, or loss or damage to property including land) is caused by a defect in a product. Strict liability does not apply to retailers.

In these circumstances, liability attaches to:

- the producer;
- anyone holding themselves out to be the producer;
- anyone importing the product into the UK as part of their business and intending to supply it to others.

A producer is the person who manufactured, abstracted or carried out an industrial process on the product. If the producer cannot be identified then each supplier of the product is to be treated as the producer unless he/she gives the injured person details of the producer or a previous supplier in the chain.

A product is defective if its safety is less than persons would be entitled to expect.

The Act permits a producer certain defences. In the absence of these circumstances, the producer will be liable without the injured person needing to prove negligence. This is the meaning of strict liability.

The defences are:

- the defect is present through compliance with EU requirements;
- the person held liable did not supply the product to anyone else;
- the product was not supplied in the course of a business;
- the defect was not in existence in the product at the relevant time;
- the scientific and technical knowledge at the time would not have revealed the defect to the producer (the 'state of the art' defence);
- the defect belonged to a subsequent product in which the original product had been put.

General Product Safety Regulations 1994

These implement EC Directive 92/59/EEC on general product safety.

Any product placed on the market must be safe, i.e. under reasonable, foreseeable conditions of use must present only the minimum of risk considered acceptable and must provide a high level of protection for health and safety risks.

Product liability policy

This was introduced to handle the risk of liability that can attach to a manufacturer, repairer or retailer of goods.

The cover provided, subject to the policy terms and conditions:

> indemnifies the insured against all sums which the insured shall become legally liable to pay as damages in respect of accidental bodily injury (including death, disease or illness) to any person or loss of or damage to material property happening anywhere in the world during the period of insurance and caused by or arising from any goods or other property and their containers (including labelling and packaging) sold supplied delivered installed erected repaired altered treated or tested by the insured from or in Great Britain, Northern Ireland, the Channel Islands or the Isle of Man in connection with the business, after they have ceased to be in the custody or control of the insured.

Only accidental loss of, or damage to, material property is covered, with financial loss covered only if consequential to the material damage.

Cover is arranged on a worldwide basis for goods exported from the insured's premises in the UK. Products liability is best arranged locally for overseas premises.

The injury or damage must normally occur during the period of insurance although claims made wordings, which cover claims actually made during the period of insurance regardless of when the loss occurred, are becoming more common.

Cover applies to injury, loss or damage caused by or arising from the goods supplied, so is not limited to the nature of the goods themselves. The goods must have ceased to be in the custody or control of the insured for cover to apply: cover should otherwise be provided under the general public liability policy.

Limit of indemnity

This is usually a yearly, total figure and includes claimants' costs and expenses.

Exclusions

Standard exclusions apply as for other liability risks:

- liability for injury to persons employed by the insured and arising out of the course of their employment: this is an employer's liability risk;
- liability in respect of loss or damage to property belonging to or in the custody or control of the insured;
- liabilities assumed by the insured under a contract that would not otherwise have applied;
- war, radioactive contamination and nuclear explosion.

Other exclusions are:

- design risks: liability arising from the design, specification or storage or use of instructions is excluded;
- repair, recall and replacement risks are excluded as the insurer is indemnifying the insured's liability to compensate those suffering injury or loss arising from the products, not the losses to the insured from defects in products;
- aviation products: are excluded because of the catastrophe risk;
- the efficacy risk where this is an important product feature (e.g. it is important that a fire alarm works properly and loss caused by its failing to do so would be excluded).

Conditions

The policy carries the following conditions:

- notification of claims: insured must report any incident that may give rise to a claim;
- claims procedures (including subrogation rights): insured gives insurer right to conduct a claim as it thinks best and to take over the insured's rights against a negligent third party;
- reasonable precautions: must be taken by the insured to prevent accidents and disease and to comply with relevant legislation;
- premium adjustment: if the premium is based on estimated figures the insured must keep accurate records and submit these so that the premium can be adjusted at the end of the period of insurance;

- other insurances: contribution clause;
- cancellation: policy may be cancelled by the insurer sending a registered letter to the insured at his or her last known address;
- observance of policy conditions: makes the observance of policy conditions precedent to liability.

Additional cover

A director or employee of a company may be prosecuted personally for an offence under the Consumer Protection Act 1987. The policy can include a clause to provide cover for the costs of conducting a defence against the prosecution.

Proposal form

A combined form is common for employer's liability, public liability and products liability risks.

Questions standard to all classes are:

- proposer's full name;
- proposer's business address;
- trade or business;
- date established;
- previous claims history;
- previous insurances.

The proposal will include a declaration to the effect that the answers given are true to the best of the proposer's knowledge and belief.

Checklist: Risk assessment

Questions specific to products liability are:

- date established: if a claims history is available it will give an indication of the past performance of the risk. New concerns and products present higher risks. The insurer will require details of the following areas with information on the intended use of the product and an estimate of 12 months' turnover for each product:

    (a) supply of products: purpose of use and estimated turnover required to help underwriter assess likelihood of a defective product giving rise to a liability and the extent of the possible injury, illness loss or damage;

(b) supply of products not manufactured: details of whether rights of recovery against the manufacturer are retained, whether the product has been adapted, the purpose of the product, the nature of the supplier and type of alteration will be required;

(c) design risks: details of any products designed, or on which advice is given or specifications prepared, and the qualifications and experience of the design staff will be required;

(d) major hazards: whether users have been warned of any hazards and what instructions are given;

(e) contractual liabilities: details of any assumed liabilities will be required;

(f) quality control: details of systems of check in operation will be required;

(g) export risks: products exported to the USA or Canada present very high risks because of the legislation in these countries and the levels of damages awarded, so the insurer will want to know about other exports, and details of products and estimated turnover;

(h) import risks: details, source and use of imported products;

(i) aircraft, marine, nuclear, offshore risks: whether products will be used in any of these industries;

(j) supply of services: are any services supplied other than the supply of products;

(k) limit of indemnity: that sought for any one accident and for any one period of insurance.

Rating

Insurers classify products and determine broad rates to apply to different trades, adjusting the rate in the light of the proposer's actual claims experience. Most split risks into:

- manufacturing, raw material suppliers and importers;
- wholesale and distribution;
- retailers;

and then classify products according to their claims potential.

The rate is then applied to the premium base, which for this class of business is usually turnover. The premium will be based on an estimate of turnover for the year, but the insured will be required to declare the actual turnover figure to the insured at the end of the period of insurance so that the premium can be adjusted accordingly. Premium levels will also be affected by the limit of liability chosen.

Risk surveys

As a complete understanding of the risk is essential, a surveyor will often be used to produce a comprehensive report for the underwriter.

Product guarantee insurance

The risks associated with the failure of a product to fulfil its intended purpose are handled by product guarantee insurance.

Product liability insurance covers liabilities in respect of bodily injury or loss of or damage to material property arising from a defect in a product, but would not cover the costs of recalling or replacing goods supplied in the absence of damage to material property.

Specific product recall policies are available but this is a specialist market and the cover is likely to be extremely costly.

Policy cover

The products guarantee policy provides cover for:

- financial loss suffered by a customer of the insured who used the defective product;
- financial loss suffered by the insured as a result of a defect in its product;
- the efficacy risk arising from a product's failure to fulfil its designed purpose or to perform to acceptable standards – pure economic loss without injury or damage is not covered;
- product recall: expenses incurred by a supplier in recalling a product or arranging its destruction. The product must be likely to cause injury or damage and the defect must result from its manufacture or design for the cover to apply;
- product replacement: limited market for costs of replacing products which have design or manufacture defects that result in the product causing injury or damage, failing to fulfil its intended function or being unsuitable for its intended purpose;
- extended warranty: cover under guarantee for a product is provided for a number of years after its purchase;
- part product: damage which one component causes to another in the same unit.

Professional indemnity insurance

Introduction

A contract between a professional and his or her client implies that reasonable care and skill will be used in the performance of the contract. If the professional fails to exercise this level of skill and care they may be negligent and if that negligence results in loss to the client, they may be sued for damages. This type of cover is sometimes referred to as 'errors and omissions'.

Professional indemnity insurance exists to protect the professional person's potential liability to pay such damages. Only legal liabilities are covered: even if a person has a moral liability to compensate a client harmed through their negligence the policy will not indemnify this liability.

The professional person is not expected to demonstrate an exceptional level of skill unless he or she is a specialist. They must exercise the degree of skill to be expected from an average member of their profession.

Since *Hedley Byrne & Co. v. Heller & Partners* (1963), a professional person can also be deemed to owe a duty of care to avoid causing a third party financial loss if giving advice that he or she might assume would be followed.

Policy cover

There is no standard wording but the policy covers the insured's legal liability for:

> damages and claimants' costs and expenses in respect of claims for breach of professional duty made against the insured and notified to the insurer during any period of insurance by reason of any neglect error or omission occurring or committed in good faith in connection with the business or practice on the part of the insured or the predecessors in the business or practice of the insured or any person (including any agent) at any time employed by the insured or such predecessors.

The claim must arise from the insured's neglect, error or omission committed in good faith – which means not dishonestly or deliberately. It must be notified to the insurer during the period of insurance for cover to apply, as policies are written on a claims made basis.

The act must be committed in connection with the business or practice on the part of the insured or any person employed by the insured or their predecessors in the business, which brings existing and future partners within the scope of the indemnity.

Partners are vicariously liable for the acts of their employees and are liable jointly and severally for acts of negligence on the part of other partners acting in the ordinary course of business. For this reason it is important that all partners are indemnified by the policy.

Limit of liability

An aggregate or total limit of liability is set for the period of insurance. Any claim within this period reduces the amount remaining available until renewal.

Claimants' costs and claim handling expenses are covered, but if the claim amount exceeds the limit of indemnity agreed under the policy, the amount paid out in respect of these costs will be the same as the ratio of the limit of indemnity and the final claim settlement.

Policies may also be subject to a single occurrence limit.

Exclusions

Risks covered by general public liability insurance are excluded, as is any claim caused by the dishonesty of the insured or their predecessors in the practice, which should be the subject of a FIDELITY INSURANCE policy.

Conditions

The policy carries the following conditions:

- notification of claims: insured must report any incident that may give rise to a claim;
- claims procedures (including subrogation rights): insured gives insurer right to conduct a claim as it thinks best and to take over the insured's rights against a negligent third party;
- reasonable precautions: must be taken by the insured to prevent

accidents and disease and to comply with relevant legislation;

- premium adjustment: if the premium is based on estimated figures the insured must keep accurate records and submit these so that the premium can be adjusted at the end of the period of insurance;
- other insurances: contribution clause;
- cancellation: policy may be cancelled by the insurer sending a registered letter to the insured at his or her last known address;
- observance of policy conditions: makes the observance of policy conditions precedent to liability.

Professional indemnity policies also commonly include a QC clause, which releases the insurer from defending an action against an insured unless a Queen's Counsel or similar authority thinks that there is a probability of success.

As a professional person's reputation is of great value to them they may wish to defend actions where objectively there is little chance of success. This clause frees the insurer from having to indemnify the insured in respect of such actions.

The insurer may also require the insured to obtain its permission before effecting additional insurance to provide a higher level of cover than available under the original policy.

Extensions

The policy may be extended to include cover for:

- breach of warranty of authority committed in good faith: a person may unknowingly exceed his or her authority to act as an agent for a third party and wish to cover any liabilities which arise in this way;
- loss of documents entrusted or deposited with the insured, subject to a limit of indemnity (e.g. £1,000);
- former partners can be indemnified by the policy;
- liabilities arising from a partner's previous business can be covered;
- a discovery period of a few months can be allowed after the end of a period of insurance, during which time a claim would be covered;
- collateral warranty cover if the professional is called upon to remedy defective work.

Cover for defamation insurance can be arranged as an extension to the professional indemnity policy rather than as a separate policy, in which case a separate limit of indemnity of perhaps 25% of the total would apply, or a fixed monetary limit, e.g. £10,000.

Checklist: Risk assessment

No standard proposal form is used, but the underwriter will be interested in the following information:

- name and address of proposer;
- profession (extensive detail required);
- date business established;
- addresses of all offices;
- details of each partner or director:

  (a) name,
  (b) age,
  (c) professional qualifications,
  (d) date qualified,
  (e) how long in practice as a partner or director;

- total number of other staff;
- previous or other professional indemnity policies;
- whether any employee has been discharged for negligence or dishonest, fraudulent, malicious or criminal conduct;
- previous professional indemnity claims made;
- any knowledge of any incident likely to give rise to a claim;
- amount of indemnity required;
- optional extensions;
- additional questions for specific professions.

Rating

Two factors influence the premium rate: the total number of people engaged in the business and the selected limit of indemnity. The rate can be increased if there are adverse features to the risk such as poor claims experience or a high ratio of partners to other staff.

The limit of indemnity should be as high as the insurer will allow – if this is still not adequate, further excess of loss cover can be arranged to secure a higher limit (see REINSURANCE).

Professional indemnity policies almost always carry significant excesses and insurers often insist that these apply to claims costs as well as to the claim, because of the cost of investigating potential claims.

Time limits for claims

The Limitation Acts impose time limits on actions for damages within which proceedings must be started. For contracts the limit is six years from the date of breach of contract, for negligence or nuisance claims six years are allowed from the date that the injury or damage was sustained.

Because of the problems that this caused people who had suffered loss or damage through negligence, but not discovered their loss until after the time limits had expired (which meant that their actions were prevented) the Latent Damage Act was passed.

This Act gives a person three years from the date on which they first had knowledge of their loss or damage to bring an action against the responsible party. It applies to actions for damages for negligence not involving personal injury.

There is a 'long-stop' date of 15 years after the date on which the alleged negligent act or omission took place, after which actions become time-barred and prevented.

For minors or disabled persons, time does not begin to run until their majority or until their disability ceases.

Professional indemnity premiums have to reflect this extended period during which claims could arise.

Professional Associations

Many professional associations impose requirements about holding professional indemnity insurance on their members, for example:

- the Institute of Chartered Accountants: minimum £50,000, maximum £500,000;
- Insurance Brokers Registration Council: minimum of £250,000 or three times annual brokerage income, whichever figure is greater;
- Personal Investment Authority: minimum £50,000.

Proposal forms

Introduction

For an underwriter to be able to assess a risk and decide on the appropriate premium for it, he or she needs access to as much information about the risk as possible and preferably to have that information presented in a way that makes assimilating it as easy as possible.

Proposal forms are the answer to this requirement for many classes of insurance, although for commercial fire risks, marine insurance risks and the placing of commercial business at Lloyd's of London they are seldom used.

Structure of forms

The proposal form for any class of business will set out clearly those questions which the underwriter particularly wants the insured to answer, designed to elicit as much information as possible about the risk to be insured.

There are certain questions that are likely to be common to all commercial insurance proposal forms:

- the name of the proposer;
- the business address and other locations to be covered;
- description of the business of the proposer;
- basis for premium calculation;
- period of cover required.

In addition, there will be a range of questions relating to the risk itself that will depend on the class of insurance concerned. The proposal form may vary in length according to the complexity of the cover to be provided.

Warning

Answers given on the proposal form will form the basis of the insurance contract. It is therefore essential that all answers given are true and complete. Non-disclosure of a material fact can render the contract void.

Declaration and important note

All proposal forms carry a declaration which must be signed by the proposer to confirm that all of the answers given are true to the best of the proposer's knowledge and belief.

The warning carried on the proposal form draws the proposer's attention to the facts that should be disclosed and to the consequences of failing to disclose facts that are material to the risk.

Placing business at Lloyd's of London

Details of risks are presented to underwriters in the Lloyd's market on 'slips'. A slip is the Lloyd's equivalent of a proposal form (though for personal lines business many syndicates do use proposal forms) and contains details of:

- the insured;
- period of cover required and date cover is to start;
- perils to be insured or type of cover sought;
- property or risk to be insured;
- sum insured or limit of liability;
- any special conditions;
- the premium sought.

If the underwriter accepts the risk, or part of the risk, he or she will stamp and initial the slip and indicate on it the proportion of the risk that they are prepared to accept. The broker may have to present the slip to a number of different underwriters until 100% of the risk has been placed.

Proximate cause

Introduction

This is an important concept in insurance policies that specify the peril against which the policy provides cover, because whether or not the policy will provide cover depends on the actual cause of the loss.

Case study

In many cases, the cause of the loss is immediately obvious.

A shop losing its stock following a break-in has evidently suffered financial loss as a result of theft.

Suppose, however, that a shop has its entire stock damaged by the operation of a sprinkler system which also manages to extinguish the small fire that triggered the sprinklers. What is the cause of the loss here? The stock wasn't burnt or smoke damaged, so would it be covered by a fire policy?

Principle of proximate cause defined

In order to decide, the principle of proximate cause needs to be applied. It was defined in the case of *Pawsey v. Scottish Union and National* (1907), as:

> the active, efficient cause that sets in motion a train of events which brings about a result without the intervention of any force started and working actively from a new and independent source.

This means that the proximate cause of a loss is the dominant cause from which a direct chain of events can be seen to lead to the loss. (Proximate means 'nearest'.)

Case study

A more visual image of this might be a line of skiers in a ski school. If a novice skier hits the end of the line and each skier in turn knocks over their neighbour, who is responsible for knocking over the person at the end of the line? Is it the person next to them, or the person who initially hit the end of the line? The principle of proximate cause would hold that the dominant cause was the skier hitting the end of the line.

However, if there was a gap between the skiers, so that only one was affected by the impact, but the person at the other side of the gap laughed so much that they lost their balance and knocked over the skier on the end of the line, that would be a new and independent cause.

In the example above, the dominant cause of the damage to the stock was the fire, the events being:

1. fire started;
2. sprinkler system operated to extinguish fire;
3. as a result of operation of sprinklers to extinguish fire, stock damaged.

If the shop owner has a policy in which fire is an insured peril, then the damage to the stock will be covered. If the insured peril is flood, then the damage would not be covered because it arose from fire.

In considering proximate cause, it is important to understand the difference between different types of peril, as the type of peril that is the proximate cause will affect the extent to which cover will be provided by the policy.

If a policy names those perils that are covered, these are known as **insured perils.**

If it also names those perils that are not covered, these are known as **excepted or excluded perils**.

Any peril that is not mentioned in the policy is known as an **unnamed** or **uninsured peril**.

If all of the events leading to the loss are insured, then it is not important to identify the proximate cause of the loss, as policy cover will automatically operate. However, if one of the events is an uninsured or an excepted peril, then it becomes important to find the proximate cause.

If the proximate cause is found to be an excepted or excluded peril, then the insurer is not liable for the loss.

If the proximate cause is an insured peril, then the insurer is liable for the loss even if the actual loss is caused by an uninsured peril.

If both an insured peril and an excluded peril led to the loss, it is essential to establish which came first. If the insured peril follows the excluded peril in unbroken sequence, the insurers have no liability.

If the excluded peril follows the insured peril, insurers are liable for damage consequent upon the operation of the insured peril, but only that incurred before the intervention of the excluded peril.

Public liability insurance

Introduction

Public liability policies protect insureds in respect of their legal liabilities to third parties for bodily injury (death, illness or disease) and loss of, or damage to, property that occurs during the period of insurance in connection with the insured business.

As public liability cover is not compulsory, the insured may incur a legal liability which, through a policy restriction or breach of a condition, the policy will not cover.

The public liability policy

The insurer will:

> indemnify the insured against legal liability to pay compensation and claimants' costs and expenses in respect of accidental:

> (a) bodily injury to any person;
> (b) loss of or damage to material property;
> (c) nuisance, trespass, obstruction or interference with any right of way, light, air or water resulting in financial loss;

> occurring within the geographical limits during the period of insurance in connection with the business.

Cover applies 'in respect of' bodily injury and therefore applies to consequential losses that result from the injury or damage. 'Accidental' means that the event must have been unexpected and not designed to happen. If the outcome of an action is not intended and could not have been foreseen as a consequence of the action, then it is accidental. A gradually operating cause is not accidental.

Injury means death, disease or illness, but can also include nervous shock. Personal injuries, such as to a person's feelings or reputation, are not covered.

Claims on the policy do not relate only to the injured third party; others may suffer loss in respect of the injury and therefore would also be covered (e.g. the third party's legal personal representatives in the event of his or her death).

The widest definition of property covers every possible interest, including goodwill and intellectual property. As insurers under public liability policies do not intend to cover these risks, reference is usually made in the policy to 'material property' or 'physical property'.

If a financial loss results from accidental nuisance, obstruction or trespass and the insured incurs a legal liability in respect of the loss, the policy will provide indemnity.

The business is identified in the policy schedule but the policy would provide cover for ancillary services. It may also cover an employee doing private work for any director, partner or employee of the insured (with the insured's permission).

Territorial limits that apply are:

- Great Britain, Northern Ireland, the Channel Islands, the Isle of Man and offshore installations around Great Britain and its continental shelf;
- any other EU country;
- elsewhere in the world by a director, partner or employee of the insured during a temporary visit if normally resident within the territorial limits.

A jurisdiction clause limiting the handling of any claim to UK legislation and scales of damages will usually be included if cover is granted outside the UK.

Limit of indemnity

There is not usually any yearly limit of indemnity imposed for a public liability policy, but a limit is set on indemnity in respect of one single accident. A common figure is £2 million; £5 million is not uncommon for larger risks.

Costs and expenses

Those costs and expenses incurred with the insurer's consent in defending a claim or representing the insured at an inquest, fatal inquiry or Court of Summary Jurisdiction are covered. Claimants' costs can either be additional to the limit of indemnity or, if the policy is written on a costs-inclusive basis, can be included within the limit.

Occurrence basis

Public liability policies have generally been written on an occurrence basis, so that for a claim to be valid the event causing it must occur during the period of insurance. However, the claims made basis, where whichever policy is in force when the claim is made meets the liability, is becoming more popular.

Exclusions

The public liability policy excludes:

- liability for injury to persons employed by the insured and arising out of the course of their employment: this is an employer's liability risk;
- liability in respect of loss or damage to property belonging to or in the custody or control of the insured;
- liability arising from the ownership, possession or use of any mechanically propelled vehicle where the Road Traffic Acts would apply: vehicles that do not have to be licensed and that are used solely on the insured's premises where there is no public right of access are covered;
- liabilities assumed by the insured under a contract which would not otherwise have applied;
- locomotives, aircraft, aerospatial devices, watercraft and hovercraft;
- advice, treatment or professional risks;
- goods sold or supplied: this is a product liability risk;
- war and radioactive contamination;
- pollution, except for that arising from sudden, unintended and unexpected causes: if the latter is covered, a limit of indemnity applies for any one period of insurance. Cover for gradually operating pollution or wider cover is provided by a separate environment impairment liability policy written on a claims made basis.

Conditions

The policy carries the following conditions:

- notification of claims: insured must report any incident that may give rise to a claim;
- claims procedures (including subrogation rights): insured gives insurer right to conduct a claim as it thinks best and to take over the insured's rights against a negligent third party;
- reasonable precautions: must be taken by the insured to prevent accidents and disease and to comply with relevant legislation;
- premium adjustment: if the premium is based on estimated figures the insured must keep accurate records and submit these so that the premium can be adjusted at the end of the period of insurance;

- other insurances: contribution clause;
- cancellation: policy may be cancelled by the insurer sending a registered letter to the insured at his or her last known address;
- observance of policy conditions: makes the observance of policy conditions precedent to liability.

It should also be noted that the following conditions apply:

- apportionment between liability insurers: if two insurers cover the same risk, any claim should be divided according to the independent liability method (see CONTRIBUTION);
- claims notification and reasonable precautions: as public liability cover is not compulsory, breach of these conditions will enable the insurer to repudiate a claim;
- discharge of liability: if a claim occurs that is higher than the single incident limit of liability, the insured may pay the amount of the limit to the insured and absolve itself from further liability (in so doing the insurer would restrict its liabilities for the payment of claimants' costs and expenses).

Checklist: Policy extensions

Standard policies can be tailored to the insured's needs, being extended or endorsed to include:

- cross liabilities clause: this prevents an insurer being liable twice to joint insureds who have separate legal liabilities;
- motor contingent liability: any risk not covered by a motor insurance policy while being driven on the insured's business but not owned by the insured would be covered;
- retrospective extension: provides claims made cover for gaps in past insurances and/or inadequate past indemnity limits;
- Defective Premises Act 1972: liabilities that may arise from defective premises owned or occupied by the insured, but not those sold, will be covered by the standard policy. This can be extended to cover premises disposed of; as the extension is usually on a claims occurring basis, a time limit (e.g. seven years) is common;
- tenants' liability: a limited amount of cover in respect of liability for loss or damage can be included.

Contractors' policy wordings

Specially worded policies are issued to meet the needs of building and civil engineering contractors. This is a specialised form of cover.

Financial loss policies

Some insurers will offer cover for liability for accidental financial loss that does not result from a physical loss or damage to material property – this is known as 'economic' loss.

Excess of loss liability policy

If a limit of liability under a particular policy is not adequate to provide the cover that an insured needs for a specific contract, a form of excess of loss cover (see REINSURANCE) can be arranged.

Proposal forms

A combined form is common for employer's liability, public liability and products liability risks, with supplementary questionnaires if information is required in greater detail.

Questions standard to all classes are:

- proposer's full name;
- proposer's business address;
- trade or business;
- date established;
- previous claims history;
- previous insurances.

The proposal will include a declaration of the answers given being true to the best of the proposer's knowledge and belief.

Questions specific to the public liability policy are:

- address of premises, public access to premises, other occupants of premises;
- mechanically propelled vehicles (not subject to the Road Traffic Act), plant hiring (in or out);
- manual work away from premises, nature of work and total estimated wages;
- contracts assuming liabilities for injury, illness, loss or damage;
- limit of indemnity required.

Rating

The most common bases for rating are wages or turnover, with premiums based on estimated amounts and a declaration of actual amounts to be made at the end of the period of insurance, so that a suitable adjustment can be made.

255

Other bases of rating used are:

- seating capacity: for public venues such as cinemas;
- membership or attendance: sports stadia;
- number of beds: nursing homes;
- number of persons engaged: small risks;
- acreage: farmers;
- gross receipts: plant hirers;
- number of pupils: schools;
- number of vehicles: haulage contractors.

A rate will be chosen to reflect the type of risk and adjusted to reflect the proposer's claims history. The limit of indemnity chosen will also affect the premium rate.

Checklist: Risk assessment

Most risks can be assessed under the headings of 'premises' and 'activities elsewhere' and the relevant considerations are:

Premises

- structure of buildings or plant;
- activities in premises;
- access and extent of third parties' presence;
- use of plant; other tenants or occupiers in premises;
- likelihood of injury to people passing the premises;
- nature of surrounding property;
- use of guard dogs.

Activities elsewhere

- loading, unloading and delivery risks;
- working on third party premises;
- working on contract sites;
- commercial travelling;
- goods stored on third party premises.

Other underwriting considerations are the risks associated with the hazards that may give rise to claims – fire, pollution, operation of equipment such as lifts, and property ownership.

The insurer will make use of a risk surveyor who will investigate closely all aspects of the risk, which will vary according to the nature of the business being undertaken.

Introduction

The main awarding bodies in the insurance industry are:

- Lloyd's of London;

- The Chartered Insurance Institute (CII);

- The Chartered Institute of Loss Adjusters (CILA);

- The Institute of Risk Management (IRM);

- The Pensions Management Institute (PMI).

Lloyd's qualifications

Lloyd's Introductory Test (LIT)

Lloyd's Market Certificate I

- LIT plus work in the Lloyd's market, plus three specified CII Associateship (ACII) subjects;
- Designatory title: None.

Lloyd's Market Certificate II

- LMCI plus five further specified ACII papers;
- Designatory title: None.

CII qualifications

Insurance Foundation Certificate (IFC)

- Two multiple choice examinations;
- Designatory title: None.

Certificate of Insurance Practice (CIP)

- Five short answer and essay examinations;
- Designatory title: Member of the Society of Technicians in Insurance (MSTI).

Associateship

- Ten essay examinations;
- Designatory title: Associate of the Chartered Insurance Institute (ACII).

Fellowship

- ACII plus three years' post-qualification experience in insurance, with satisfactory evidence of professional development, plus dissertation;
- Designatory title: Fellow of the Chartered Insurance Institute (FCII).

Financial Planning Certificate (FPC)

- One case study-based and two multiple choice examinations;
- Designatory title: None.

Advanced Financial Planning Certificate (AFPC)

- Three essay examinations;
- Designatory title: Member of the Society of Financial Advisers (MSFA).

SOFA qualifications

Associateship

- Six essay examinations plus three years' relevant experience and recorded continuous professional development for one year;
- Designatory title: Associate of the Society of Financial Advisers (ASFA).

Fellowship

- Ten essay examinations plus five years' relevant experience and recorded CPD for three years;
- Designatory title: Fellow of the Society of Financial Advisers (FSFA).

CILA qualifications

Certificate of Adjusting Procedures

- Three examinations;
- Designatory title: None.

Associateship

- CII ACII or equivalent qualification plus seven essay examinations;
- Designatory title: Associate of the Chartered Institute of Loss Adjusters (ACILA).

Institute of Risk Management qualifications

Graduate

- Must have qualified in Risk Management;
- Designatory title: Graduate of the Institute of Risk Management (GRAD IRM).

Associateship

- Five compulsory examinations, one optional;
- Designatory title: Associate of the Institute of Risk Management (AIRM).

Fellowship

- AIRM plus dissertation, plus five years' minimum work experience;
- Designatory title: Fellow of the Institute of Risk Management (FIRM).

PMI qualifications

Associateship

- Nine exams plus minimum three years' practical work in pensions;
- Designatory title: Associate of the Pensions Management Institute (APMI).

Fellowship

- APMI plus eight years' full practical experience;
- Designatory title: Fellow of the Pensions Management Institute (FPMI).

Regulation

Introduction

Legislation constitutes the main form of regulation for insurance business in the UK, with the codes of conduct of professional associations supplementing the legislation.

Insurance Companies Act 1982

The Department of Trade and Industry (DTI) is responsible for the regulation of insurance companies in the UK under the Insurance Companies Act 1982 (see separate section). It grants authorisation to write insurance only to those companies which it considers are operated by fit and proper people and imposes solvency margins and accounting requirements to ensure that sufficient assets exist to meet an insurer's liabilities at all times.

Policyholders Protection Act 1975

This established the Policyholders Protection Board, which through a levy on insurance companies ensures that funds are available to meet an insured's claim if their insurance company becomes insolvent and unable to fulfil its responsibilities to policyholders.

Claims under compulsory insurance covers such as motor or employer's liability would be met in full in these circumstances, while 90% of the value of other claims would be provided.

Claims for marine, aviation, transit and reinsurance risks are not covered, nor are claims from companies under general insurance policies.

Insurance Brokers (Registration) Act 1977

Since the introduction of this Act, only those INTERMEDIARIES who are registered with the body set up under the Act, the Insurance Brokers Registration Council, can use the title 'insurance broker'.

The IBRC has responsibility for the registration and regulation of insurance brokers.

The main provisions of the Act are:

- the registration of insurance brokers: the IBRC must register all those who want to call themselves insurance brokers and ensure that they meet the qualifications for registration;
- the regulation of the conduct of brokers: brokers must follow the IBRC code of conduct, meet the IBRC requirements for carrying out business, hold the required level of professional indemnity insurance and contribute to the Grants Scheme;
- disciplinary procedures: a broker can be struck off the IBRC register by the disciplinary committee;
- restriction on the use of titles and descriptions: anyone wilfully using the title 'insurance broker' while not registered can be fined on each occasion of use.

The qualifications for registration with the IBRC are that a broker:

- holds an approved qualification (the Associateship or Fellowship of the Chartered Insurance Institute); or
- has been employed (or carried on business) as a broker for at least five years or has equivalent experience of the insurance business; or
- holds a recognised qualification and had three years' experience as a broker or in the insurance business.

Financial Services Act 1986

This Act was passed to regulate the activities of those selling investment products. It requires that anyone engaged in investment business must be authorised or exempt and imposes rules on how authorised persons conduct their business.

All long-term insurances (life assurances and pensions) are covered by the FSA, as are all other investment products such as stocks and shares, debentures, loan stocks, bonds and unit trusts.

Authorisation can be obtained either from the Securities and Investments Board which was set up to oversee the working of the requirements of the Act or, more usually, from one of the self-regulating organisations (SROs) or recognised professional bodies (RPBs) such as the IBRC, the Institute of Actuaries and the various Institutes of Chartered Accountants, to whom SIB has delegated powers to authorise.

There are currently three SROs:

- the Personal Investment Authority, which regulates independent financial advisers, company representatives and appointed representatives (tied agents). The PIA took over the membership of two previous SROs, LAUTRO, which represented the product providers, and FIMBRA, which represented the independent financial advisers;

- the Investment Management Regulatory Organisation (IMRO), which regulates the managers of investments;
- the Securities and Futures Association (SFA), which regulates market makers, futures and options dealers, stockbrokers and securities dealers.

Codes of Practice

These are adopted and followed voluntarily by the members of the organisations that produce them.

Association of British Insurers

The ABI produces a number of codes of practice for general and long-term business. These are discussed in the separate section on the ABI.

Insurance Brokers' Registration Council

This applies to all insurance brokers registered with the IBRC, and sets out a professional standard of conduct that all brokers should meet. The most recent code was released in 1994 and contains eight basic principles for brokers to follow.

Checklist: IBRC code of conduct

Brokers must:

- at all times carry out business with paramount faith and integrity;
- do everything possible to satisfy the clients' requirements;
- do nothing to damage the reputation of insurance brokers or the overall profession;
- ensure that advertising is not misleading or exaggerated;
- show propriety in their relationship with the IBRC;
- manage their business responsibly and ensure that staff are competent, suitable and properly supervised;
- be aware of guidance as to proper professional conduct in Council Practice Notes; and
- if authorised to conduct relevant investment business, comply with any statements of principle issued under Section 47A of the Financial Services Act 1986.

The Code gives brokers over 30 examples of the application of these principles.

Lloyd's of London

As provided under the Lloyd's Act 1982, Lloyd's operates a system of self-regulation, in that it devises, and ensures compliance with, its own rules. The purpose of the regulatory system at Lloyd's is:

- to maintain the security of the Lloyd's policy;
- to maintain the highest standards of conduct and integrity amongst all in the Lloyd's market;
- to preserve Lloyd's as a freely competitive market;
- to maintain standards of fair treatment for all Lloyd's members.

The structure and regulation of Lloyd's is discussed in the separate LLOYD'S OF LONDON section.

Reinsurance

Introduction

In the same way as a person may wish to transfer the risk of a loss to an insurer for the financial security and peace of mind that this brings, an insurer which has accepted a risk from an insured may wish to transfer that risk on to someone else for its own financial security.

This process of insuring a risk that is already insured is known as reinsurance.

Parties to the contract

The contract of reinsurance is between the direct insurer which has accepted the risk from the insured, and the reinsurer. There is no contractual relationship between the insured under the initial policy and the reinsurer. The insurer remains fully liable to the insured for any losses under the policy, but it will then recover part or all of its own outlay from the reinsurer.

The insurer has insurable interest in the risk being reinsured because of its liability to indemnify the insured in the event of an insured loss.

Checklist: Reinsurance terminology

Reinsurance uses some different phrases to the rest of the insurance market:

- the insurer that accepts the initial risk is known as the *direct insurer;*
- the risk to be reinsured is known as a *cession* and *'to cede'* means to pass on the risk to the reinsurer. Because of this, the direct insurer is also known as the *ceding company;*
- the ceding company decides how much of each risk it wants to reinsure and how much it is going to retain. This amount is its *retention.*

Types of reinsurance

Reinsurance is arranged on either a facultative or a treaty basis.

Facultative reinsurance

If an insurer offers each risk to a reinsurer, which decides whether or not it wishes to offer reinsurance on the risk and if so, at what terms, this is facultative reinsurance. The insurer has no obligation to pass on risks to the reinsurer and the reinsurer has no obligation to accept any risks offered. Each risk placed is subject to a separate contract.

Treaty reinsurance

Alternatively, the insurer can enter into a binding contract or treaty with one or more reinsurers whereby the reinsurer must accept all risks falling within the terms agreed for the treaty, and the direct insurer must cede all such risks. Neither the insurer nor the reinsurer have any knowledge at the outset of the risks that will ultimately form part of the treaty.

Treaty reinsurance is the more popular form as there is less administration involved, the insurer knows that it has reinsurance cover available to it before accepting a risk and the treaty provides better results for the reinsurer as all risks, not just those where the experience is expected to be poor, are reinsured.

Types of treaty reinsurance

Treaty reinsurance can take various forms, depending on the needs of the insurer. Treaties are either written on a proportional basis, or a non-proportional basis.

Proportional reinsurance:

In proportional treaties, the insurer decides how much to reinsure and the balance is then reinsured under the treaty. The premium received by the direct insurer for the risk is shared in the same proportion as the retention bears to the reinsurance, between the insurer and the reinsurer. Any losses that also occur under the policy will be shared in the same proportion.

- **quota share**: the treaty reinsures a fixed proportion of any risk falling within its terms, receiving a proportional amount of the premium and paying out a proportional amount of the losses;
- **surplus**: the insurer decides on a monetary amount as its retention and then reinsures under the treaty any amounts that exceed this figure.

The treaty is arranged in 'lines', with each line being a sum equal to the insurer's retention. A five-line treaty would provide reinsurance cover of five times the insurer's retention. A treaty will have a maximum limit of lines, but if the insurer wishes to accept risks with a greater value than the treaty can accommodate, then further surplus treaties can be arranged.

Non-proportional reinsurance:

In non-proportional treaties, the insurer and reinsurer agree on a level of loss and the treaty then provides reinsurance cover for any losses that occur beyond that level.

- **excess of loss**: under this type of treaty, the insurer and reinsurer agree on the amount that the insurer is to retain. If losses under the policy remain within this limit, the reinsurer does not become involved, but if the loss exceeds the amount agreed the reinsurer is liable to pay the balance, up to another agreed limit. Excess of loss treaties are arranged in layers, with different layers being called upon as a claim moves from one layer into the next. The first layer, which is most likely to be called upon, is known as the working layer and is the most costly to put in place;
- **excess of loss ratio (stop loss)**: this type of treaty is designed to protect the insurer's whole account from higher than expected losses. It pays out when the loss ratio (total losses divided by total premiums) on the insurer's account exceeds a certain percentage. Like other treaties, there is a ceiling placed on the reinsurer's liability.

For non-proportional reinsurances, the premium is likely to be based on a rate applied to the premiums from the direct insurances, calculated to cover the reinsurer's costs and to cover expenses, contingencies, profit and brokerage, the commission paid to the broker who places the treaty with the reinsurer.

Renewals

Introduction

Insurance policies are issued for a particular term, which can be for three months, a year, or a person's lifetime, depending on the type of policy involved.

By far the most policies are issued for a period of one year. At the end of this time, the insurer will decide whether it wishes to invite renewal of the policy and the insured will have to decide whether or not to accept the renewal invitation.

Renewal terms

The terms offered to the insured at renewal will depend upon the experience of the policy during the previous term. If there have been no claims and no other changes have been made to the risk, then renewal is likely to be offered on the same terms as the previous year (although premium rates may have increased slightly to keep pace with inflation). It costs insurers a lot less to renew a policy than to take out a new policy and consequently they are keen to encourage insureds to renew.

Renewal notice

The insurer will normally issue a renewal notice, drawing to the insured's attention the fact that renewal is due and making it as easy as possible for the insured to renew the policy. If the insured returns the necessary premium to renew the policy, then confirmation of renewal will be issued, together with a certificate of insurance where this is a feature of the insurance cover.

Days of grace

If the renewal premium is not paid by renewal date, the policy will lapse. However, in recognition of the fact that an insured can intend to renew a policy but fail to get the premium to the insured by renewal date, insurers of some classes of business permit what are known as 'days of grace' at renewal. If the premium is paid during the days of grace (usually 15 to 30 days) cover will be permitted to continue from the original renewal date, with no break.

Motor insurance

It is a legal requirement to have valid motor insurance before using a motor vehicle on a public road. It is also a criminal offence to backdate cover.

To deal with the insured's need for continuous cover and the possibility that there may be some delay in the renewal premium reaching the insurer, the insurer includes a 15-day certificate with the renewal documentation. This provides the insured with the minimum legal cover if the premium is not paid by the due date. However, it will only provide cover for the insured if the policy is renewed within the term of the temporary certificate – if the policy lapses and the insured takes out a policy a week later with another insurer, then he will have been without any motor insurance cover for that week and will have committed a criminal offence if he has driven the car during that time. The case law on this subject also indicates that the insured must have been aware of the existence of this 15-day certificate and have intended to rely upon it. If he was not aware of its existence, then the policy would be deemed to have lapsed on renewal date.

Long-term agreements

Insurers may sometimes offer a discount to the insured in return for an agreement that the insured will renew the policy for a set period of time. A discount of 5% could therefore be enjoyed by an insured who agrees to renew the policy for three years. Both sides benefit from this arrangement.

Duty of disclosure

As renewal actually involves the creation of a new contract of insurance, both parties to the contract have the same responsibilities at renewal as they had at inception – to disclose any material fact that may be relevant to the risk. At renewal, this means particularly any material changes in the risk since the inception of the policy or the last renewal date. Failure to disclose material information at renewal can invalidate the policy cover.

Risk management

Introduction

There are three aspects to risk management:

- identification;

- analysis;

- control.

Risk identification

This process looks objectively at a business and considers the full range of events that could prevent it from achieving its objectives.

This task falls within the responsibilities of a risk manager if the business has one, but otherwise is part of the responsibilities shared by the business's senior management. Insurers, through the process of risk surveys, can assist in identifying risks although risks also exist that are beyond the scope of insurance and a business must not overlook these.

Identification tools

These can be used to assist in the identification of risk:

- organisation charts: provide an overview of the structure of a company, and can reveal areas of risk concentration or possible dependencies between different business areas;
- physical inspections: it is useful to plan a structure for the inspection and to have a structured format for recording information;
- checklists: if the person identifying the risk is not based at the premises, a checklist can be produced for completion by someone on site – care must be taken in the drafting and structuring of a checklist if it is to elicit all of the information required;
- flow charts: pictorial representations of stages in a flow of business activities, whether a process or the flow of something like money, which can reveal areas of potential risk;
- hazard and operability studies (HAZOPs): extremely detailed

examinations of a plant or process, commonly used in high-risk industries where areas of general risk are already known, but specialised risk analysis is being undertaken;

- fault trees: these start from potential risks and trace backwards the range of events and sequences of events that could result in the risk occurring.

Whichever method is chosen, risk identification should be an ongoing responsibility and should involve the production of comprehensive records that can provide the basis for future risk assessment.

Risk analysis

Once risks have been identified, their possible impact on a business must be analysed so that decisions can be made about how to handle the risk.

Statistical analysis can be employed to evaluate the likely level of frequency or severity of a risk event.

Before any decisions are made, the analysis of the level of risk present must be taken into account. If a risk has been identified, but is likely to cost at most £10 if it occurs, it would not make good economic sense to spend £100 to remove that risk. Once a value has been demonstrated in controlling risk, then means can be taken to achieve that control.

Risk control

Once the extent of possible risk has been identified, the last part of the process of risk management is to seek possible ways of controlling it.

Physical risk control

This applies in two phases, pre- and post-loss. Pre-loss measures consider and take action to prevent the risk occurring, such as installing safety guards on machinery, while post-loss measures imagine the risk occurring and then ask what could be done to minimise its impact, such as installing sprinkler systems and fire-resistant walls to minimise the impact and spread of fire.

Financial risk control

Here there are two further options, risk retention and risk transfer. If the business decides to retain the risk, it is wise to set aside funds to deal with the consequences should the risk occur; otherwise costs would have to be met from operating funds, which could place a severe financial strain on the business. If it decides to transfer risk, the main option available is to effect the appropriate insurance cover.

Warning

In evaluating whether to self-insure or to take out insurance, those responsible should try to compare the cost of the likely effect of the risk with likely premiums if insurance is effected externally.

The insurance manager should not make a decision of this scale without guidelines or a set of criteria from senior management that identify the acceptable level of risk.

Self-insurance

Introduction

If a company has fairly predictable losses, then it may decide to self-insure. Self-insurance may also be necessary if a company cannot find an insurer willing to offer the cover it requires.

To self-insure, the company would set up a fund from which all losses of a particular sort would be paid. The size of the fund would depend on the size of the company and the type of losses that the fund would cover, although it would need to be quite large to cover all eventualities.

By self-insuring, the company saves money which it would otherwise have spent on premiums. The choice of self-insurance is most appropriate for losses that occur frequently, but are not of high severity.

Case study

Suppose a company has a fleet of delivery vehicles. The accidental damage risk to those vehicles would probably be fairly expensive to insure because it is relatively frequent and yet it would never give rise to a single loss of more than the replacement cost of the vehicle itself. This could therefore present a suitable opportunity for self-insurance.

However, the same company would probably not choose to self-insure the third party liability risk for the same fleet, because the potential losses could be so much higher. (Imagine a delivery vehicle crashing into a shop and seriously injuring two people who could never work again – the cost of this one incident would exhaust a small fund and could force the company to close.)

In order to make a balanced decision, it is important to collect information on all incidents, not just those which give rise to claims on existing policies.

Non-insurance

Self-insurance represents a conscious, balanced decision to set up a fund for specific losses. Companies that self-insure are very different from those that simply intend to meet any losses out of future profits. These latter are non-insurers, putting in place no arrangements at all to deal with future losses, but hoping that they will have sufficient money at the time to deal with their losses and liabilities.

Today, self-insurance is almost invariably done through a captive company (see INSURANCE COMPANIES).

Subrogation

Introduction

If a person causes you injury or loss, you have certain legal rights to recover the amount of your loss, or damages in respect of your injury, from them. The courts uphold these rights.

If, however, you have insurance, then your insurer will provide you with the necessary compensation for your injury or loss.

Theoretically, you could recover this amount twice, once from the third party responsible and once from your insurer.

Indemnity

Insurance contracts (for non-life business) are contracts of INDEMNITY, which means that a person should recover the exact amount of their loss, no more and no less. Indemnity thus rules out a person recovering twice for the same loss.

Principle of subrogation

Subrogation is closely linked to the principle of indemnity. If an injured person claims on an insurance policy, then the third party responsible for the injury has avoided their responsibility if the insurer indemnifies its insured. To avoid this situation, the principle of subrogation passes the right to the insurer, once it has paid its insured's claim, to pursue any rights that the insured may have had to recover compensation from the third party.

Case study

A woman driving to work is hit from behind by a third party who was not paying attention and who failed to notice that the traffic lights had changed to red. The woman's car is severely damaged and her passenger suffers whiplash injuries to her neck.

The woman has a comprehensive motor insurance policy. Her insurer pays for repairs to her car and settles her passenger's claim in respect of her injuries.

In order to reduce its own outlay, the insurer then takes action in the insured's name against the responsible third party, eventually recovering the cost of the repairs to the car and the amount of the injury settlement. Note that if the insurer recovers from the third party more than it has paid out to the insured, it may not keep the difference, which must be returned to the insured.

This is an example of how subrogation would work at common law.

Subrogation condition

At common law, the insurer must have indemnified the insured before it can take over the insured's rights against a third party. Insurance policies therefore include what is known as the subrogation condition, which gives the insurer the right to begin actions to recover against a third party as soon as their insured notifies them of a claim.

This is helpful to insurers because it enables them to start investigating the circumstances of the incident giving rise to the claim while it is still fresh in the minds of the people involved and of any witnesses.

Subrogation rights

These can arise:
- *in tort:* where a person fails to act in a reasonable way and causes injury to someone else;
- *in contract:* where a person breaches a contract and losses result;
- *in statute:* where insurers may sue in their own names for compensation paid to the insured in respect of damages caused by a riot as defined by the Riot (Damages) Act 1886.

Terrorism cover

Introduction

Cover originally provided by reinsurance companies in respect of damage caused by terrorism was withdrawn after the bombs at St Mary Axe and Bishopsgate in London in the early 1990s.

Provision of cover

After 1992, the ABI decided to exclude terrorism risks from commercial and industrial property policies. There is a terrorism exclusion incorporated in fire and special perils policies, which excludes all damage arising from terrorism except that covered to a limited extent by the Special Provision – Terrorism.

The recommended exclusion wording permits cover to be 'bought back' up to prescribed limits. Prescribed premium rates apply, or special rates if risks are targets needing individual underwriting. Cover relates to mainland Great Britain for non-domestic property and related risks (e.g. business interruption).

Insurers felt able to continue to provide cover for terrorism on request, as the government decided to act as insurer of last resort.

Premiums are determined by reference to a rating tariff, which splits risks into four zones, each with its own rating. If cover is required an insured must insure all of its premises – it cannot select only those most likely to be targeted.

A specially created company, Pool Reinsurance Company Limited, was set up to offer cover up to specified limits. Membership of Pool Re is voluntary but members must cede 100% of covers into the pool.

The primary insurer is responsible for the first £100,000 of any commercial risk and for the whole amount of any domestic risk.

Special Provision – Terrorism

Cover is provided for damage by fire or explosion in England, Wales and Scotland caused by terrorism.

The liability of the insurer is limited to whichever is the lower of:

- £100,000 per loss occurrence except for buildings or blocks of flats occupied exclusively as private dwellings;
- £2.5 million per loss occurrence for buildings or blocks of flats occupied exclusively as private dwellings; or
- any limit of liability stated in the policy.

Cover provided relates to buildings and other property, business interruption and book debts.

Government intervention

If there are not enough funds in the pool to pay claims, the first step is to call on the insurers of the risks in the pool to add further funds on the basis of 10% of the premiums collected from their policyholders.

If claims still exceed the funds available, the balance will be paid by the government.

Theft insurance

Introduction

The Theft Act 1968 introduced the following definitions for theft, robbery and burglary.

Theft

(1) A person is guilty of theft if he dishonestly appropriates property belonging to another with the intention of permanently depriving the other of it; and 'thief' and 'steal' shall be construed accordingly.

(2) It is immaterial whether the appropriation is made with a view to gain or is made for the thief's own benefit.

Robbery

A person is guilty of robbery if he steals, and immediately before or at the time of doing so, and in order to do so, he uses force on any person or puts or seeks to put any person in fear of being then and there subjected to force.

Burglary

(1) A person is guilty of burglary if:

    (a) he enters any building or part of a building as a trespasser and with intent to commit any such offence as is mentioned in subsection (2) below: or

    (b) having entered any building or part of a building as a trespasser he steals or attempts to steal anything in the building or that part of it or inflicts or attempts to inflict on any person therein any grievous bodily harm.

(2) The offences referred to in subsection (1)(a) above are offences of stealing anything in the building or part of a building in question, of inflicting on any person therein any grievous bodily harm or raping any woman therein, and of doing unlawful damage to the building or anything therein.

Policy cover

The theft policy has always been intended to exclude cover for people who may be lawfully on premises, as this risk is better covered by a FIDELITY INSURANCE policy or would relate to a risk such as shoplifting which would be undesirable because of its frequency.

The wording often used, although there is no standard policy wording in use, provides cover for: 'Theft involving entry to or exit from the premises by forcible and violent means.'

This is a restricted cover, which would exclude claims from anyone on the premises through use of a key; trickery or hiding on the premises until they are closed for business, unless they used force or violence to make their escape.

An even more restricted wording would cover: 'Theft following forcible and violent entry.'

The policy defines what is meant by certain terms:

- premises: buildings at the address in the schedule occupied by the insured in connection with its business, but excluding gardens, yards, open spaces or outbuildings;
- stock: stock and materials belonging to the insured or held in trust and for which the insured is responsible;
- business equipment: trade equipment, fixtures, fittings, machinery, plant and all other contents excluding stock;
- all other contents: belonging to or held in trust by the insured. These can be deeds, documents or business books; computer systems records; patterns, models, moulds, plans and designs; directors' and employees' clothing, personal effects and pedal cycles up to a limited amount per person.

The policy provides the following indemnity:

If during the period of insurance:

(1) any of the property while within the premises shall be lost, damaged or destroyed as a result of:

    (a) theft, or attempted theft, involving entry to or exit from the premises by forcible and violent means; or

    (b) theft following assault or violence or threat thereof to the insured or any director, partner or employee of the insured; or

(2) the premises shall sustain damage for which the insured is responsible, as a result of theft or attempted theft, involving entry to or exit from the premises by forcible and violent means.

Then the company will by payment, or at its option, by repair, replacement or reinstatement indemnify the insured in respect of such loss or damage to the extent of and subject to the terms and conditions of this policy.

The cover provided is quite clear, the insured will be indemnified for any property stolen under the terms of the policy and for any damage to property resulting from theft.

A limit of liability will be agreed for:

- every item of property shown in the policy schedule;
- for making good damage to premises;
- the total loss or damage insured under the policy.

Checklist: Policy extensions

Theft insurers offer automatic policy extensions that appear as part of the cover for the most part, but may sometimes be provided in return for the payment of an additional premium:

- index linking: as for household contracts, sums insured can be index-linked and adjusted on a monthly basis to cover the effects of inflation;
- temporary removal: costs involved in removing items temporarily for cleaning or repair;
- breakage of glass: if glass insurance is not otherwise held by the insured;
- replacement of locks: resulting from loss of keys or theft of keys from the premises.

Optional extensions include:

- first loss cover (see separate section);
- cover for losses resulting from collusion;
- extended or fuller description of theft, widening the cover provided;
- claims to be settled on a reinstatement as new basis;
- sums insured to be reinstated to the original value following a claim;
- voluntary excess to gain discounted premium;
- stock declaration throughout the year;
- wider wording of theft cover for hotels, which never really close for business.

Exclusions

Risks excluded by the theft policy are:

- collusion: cover can be bought back (included) by payment of an extra premium;
- fire and explosion: if otherwise covered under a fire and special perils insurance;
- war risks: the standard exclusion;
- ionising radiation or radioactive contamination: the standard exclusion.

Property excluded under the theft policy:

- money and other securities;
- livestock.

Conditions

These are common to other material damage policies:

- alteration: the insured must notify the insurer of any alteration to the risk;
- reasonable precautions: the insured is responsible for taking due care of the property;
- action by the insured: sets out the things that an insured must do in the event of a claim;
- fraud: any fraud invalidates the policy cover;
- contribution (see separate section);
- cancellation;
- average (underinsurance) (see separate section).

Warranties

The theft policy is likely to carry WARRANTIES, which aim to ensure that the insured behaves in a particular way if cover is to apply. Common warranties would relate to the installation and operation of intruder alarms and to the security arrangements for safe or strongroom keys.

Insurers may also insist on particular forms of security protection being put in place before they are prepared to offer cover on the risk.

Rating

The factors that an underwriter would use in rating a theft insurance risk are essentially the nature of the insured's trade and the product or commodity to be insured, and the location of the premises.

The hazards associated with a particular trade are of less significance to theft insurers, who are concerned with the attractiveness of the stock to be covered to potential thieves.

Insurers are likely to use a classification system for different trades, with the least hazardous trades such as booksellers or furniture dealers in Class 1, medium risks such as cycle dealers, grocers and photographers in Class 2 and high-risk trades in Class 3, for example: clothes retailers, photographic retailers, television, entertainment systems or computer dealers and sports and leather goods dealers.

Losses can be statistically linked to particular areas and therefore the location of the premises to be insured is of great importance. District codes may be used to indicate the rates to apply to each area, or some insurers may now base rates on different postal codes for even greater rating sophistication.

The premium quoted will be a combination of these two factors, producing a rate that can be applied to the sum insured to give the premium.

Checklist: Risk assessment

It is important for the theft insurer to have information on each of the following areas in order to be able to assess the amount of risk presented by the proposal:

- moral hazard: this is of prime importance with this class of insurance;
- security: the insurer may impose specific security levels on the insured as a condition of offering cover;
- occupancy: whether or not a building is regularly occupied by the insured's employees can have a significant impact on reducing its attractiveness as a target for theft;
- construction: buildings that are securely constructed will present a much better risk than those of lightweight construction;
- loss history: this will reveal a lot about the moral hazard relating to the risk – if the loss history is poor, the insurer may decline the risk, require improvement in aspects of the risk before offering cover, or impose premium loadings and increased compulsory excesses.

Additional notice will be taken of whether a scaled rating structure is to apply, with 100% of the premium applying to the underwriter's estimation of a maximum probable loss and lesser proportions of the premium applying to smaller loss figures.

Risks that involve a mixture of goods of different attractiveness are handled by splitting the rating to reflect the different aspects of the risk; for insureds with a number of premises to be insured no strict rules apply, with most insurers rating each location as a separate risk.

Computer equipment

This poses particular problems as it is increasingly targeted by thieves to whom the easy disposal and high values paid for the microprocessor chips stolen from within the hardware are very attractive.

Whereas office premises were traditionally considered to be low risk, if computer equipment is to be covered the insurers would probably insist on at least one of the following measures being taken:

- full inventory of electronic equipment kept, with information on make, model and serial numbers;
- ultra-violet marking or security tagging for ease of identification;
- quality locks on all windows and doors;
- suitable alarm protection;
- lock down plates to prevent equipment being moved and locking back plates to prevent access to the chips;
- use of security guards outside office hours;
- access control.

Travel insurance

Introduction

Most travel insurance policies provide cover for three months, although annual policies are available for those who travel frequently.

Policy cover

Cover is normally provided under the following headings:

Personal accident benefits

In the event of death, loss of limbs or eyes (or eyesight) or permanent total disablement a lump sum payment will be made to insured or to their legal personal representatives. The amount is generally between £10,000 and £25,000. It is possible for a policy to include a weekly paid benefit for temporary total or partial disablement.

The policy will exclude losses arising from the insured's taking part in hazardous pastimes, unless an additional premium is paid to cover these.

Medical expenses

The policy will cover expenses incurred in respect of:

- medical treatment: hospital charges, surgical fees, emergency dental treatment;
- additional hotel or travelling expenses: incurred as a result of the patient's accident or illness, by the patient or by a member of their family, friend or nurse travelling with them;
- repatriation costs: including the use of an air ambulance if necessary;
- additional expenses incurred by others in the insured's party: to cover costs associated with delay as a result of the illness (limit of £250 common).

A sum insured of £2 million is usual, but this is for overseas travel; within the UK where the National Health Service is available, the limit is likely to be much less, closer to £1,000.

Loss of deposits

If the insured's holiday has to be cancelled unavoidably because of:

- their death, illness or accident, or that of any person with whom they were intending to travel, or of a relative or close business associate;
- their being called to jury service or as a witness;
- being made redundant with no prior notification;
- their workload preventing them taking holiday;
- theft or fire at their home or at work;

then the policy will provide for their deposits and payments in respect of transport and accommodation to be returned. It is important that the cancellation is a direct result of one of these reasons and not just the insured changing their mind about the holiday.

Baggage, personal effects and money

Loss of, or damage to personal baggage, clothing and personal effects is covered, up to a common limit of £2,000. A lesser limit would apply to single articles (e.g. £250) and to valuables (e.g. £500). A small excess will also apply.

These limits can be increased if necessary.

Loss of money (cash, notes, travellers' cheques, travel tickets etc.) would be covered up to £500, or more if the policy is to include cover for credit cards and passports.

Personal liability

If the insured incurs a legal liability in respect of injury to a third party or accidental loss of, or damage to, their property whilst travelling then the insurer will indemnify the insured up to a limit, which is between £500,000 and £1 million.

Delayed baggage

If baggage is delayed for more than 12 hours, a small amount of cover is available for essential items of clothing and toiletries.

Hospital cash benefits

A small amount is provided to the insured whilst confined to hospital: £10 – £15 per day, subject to a limit of between £200 and £600.

Travel interruption

Cost of additional accommodation and travel is covered up to £300 if the public transport system fails to deliver the insured to the departure point in time to take the trip on either the inward or outward journey.

Travel delay

If the aircraft or ship is delayed for more than 12 hours, a small amount, e.g. £20, is payable for each further 12-hour delay.

Optional extensions

Cover may also be included for:

- financial failure of the tour organiser: as long as the tour operator is a member of or licensed by the Association of British Travel Agents, the Civil Aviation Authority or another appropriate body;
- lack of services or amenities: if there is a substantial lack of services at a hotel where the insured is staying as a result of industrial action lasting for more than 48 hours, a small amount of compensation can be provided;
- loss of passport: up to £250 in respect of the costs of obtaining a passport to replace one lost or stolen;
- legal expenses: cover for the costs of pursuing claims for compensation arising out of the death or injury of the insured (up to £25,000).

Exclusions

The policy excludes:

- death, bodily injury or sickness:

  (a) caused by unprescribed drugs or intoxicants;
  (b) due to insanity, pregnancy or childbirth;
  (c) resulting from any physical or mental defect;
  (d) while taking part in any hazardous activity;
  (e) from suicide or self-inflicted injury;
  (f) attributable to HIV or AIDS;

- loss of:

  (a) luggage through confiscation;
  (b) stamps, manuscripts or documents;
  (c) camping equipment;

(d) cash and cheques unless reported to the police within 24 hours;

- damage to fragile objects.

Rating

This depends on the geographical areas to be visited, with most insurers offering different rates to include:

- the United Kingdom only;
- Europe and Mediterranean countries (except Egypt, Jordan, Lebanon, Libya, Israel and Syria), Madeira and the Canary Islands;
- worldwide except for North America, the West Indies, the Bahamas and Bermuda;
- worldwide.

Underwriter

Introduction

The underwriter is the person who decides whether or not a risk should be accepted by an insurance company, and if it is to be accepted, what rates, terms and conditions should apply.

Origin

Originally, details of marine risks would be presented to people likely to take a share of the insurance on the hull or the cargo involved. Because the person who agreed to carry the risk signed his name under the details of the risk, in time the term 'underwriter' came to be applied to those persons who accepted insurance risks.

Functions

It is the underwriter's main responsibility to manage the common insurance pool into which all premiums go, and from which all claims are made, to ensure that each risk accepted contributes an amount to the pool that matches the risk of loss.

In order to achieve this, the underwriter must:

- assess the risk being brought to the pool;
- decide whether or not to accept part or all of the risk;
- specify what cover must apply to the policy and any terms and conditions that must be imposed; and
- calculate an appropriate premium to reflect the amount of risk being brought to the pool.

The underwriter will wish to have as much information about the risk proposed as possible to assist in the process of decision-making.

Utmost good faith

Introduction

The proposer and the insurer both have a duty to behave with utmost good faith (the Latin phrase is *uberrima fides*) when negotiating a contract of insurance.

Obligations of utmost good faith

This means that each party must voluntarily inform the other of all facts that are relevant (material) to the contract being negotiated. The information provided must be as complete and as accurate as possible. Utmost good faith imposes a duty to supply the information whether the other party asks for it or not.

Lord Justice Scrutton made this principle explicit in his statement in *Rozanes v. Bowen* (1928):

> As the underwriter knows nothing and the man who comes to him to ask him to insure knows everything, it is the duty of the assured . . . to make a full disclosure to the underwriter without being asked of all the material circumstances. This is expressed by saying it is a contract of the utmost good faith.

For a more detailed discussion of material facts, see DUTY OF DISCLOSURE.

Warranties

Introduction

An insurer will sometimes wish to make an insured promise to do or not do something during the term of the policy. This is a warranty. A warranty can also be a promise made by the insured in respect of the truth of facts provided about the risk.

Essentially, a warranty is an undertaking given by the insured that something will be done (or will not be done) or that a particular state of affairs exists (or does not exist).

Warranties can relate to present and past situations or to future situations, in which case they are known as continuing warranties.

Types of warranty

Warranties can be either express or implied.

Express warranties

Express warranties are specified in the policy, and place a responsibility on the insured. Examples in theft insurance could include the requirement that approved locks and security devices would be fitted, and in property insurance that waste would be removed at the end of each day's operations. An example of a wording used in fire insurance would be:

> It is warranted that all fire break doors and shutters will be kept closed except during working hours and will be maintained in efficient working order.

Implied warranties

Implied warranties are not written into the policy but would be understood by both parties to apply to the contract. They are only encountered in marine insurance, where the seaworthiness of the vessel to be insured is an implied warranty in any marine insurance contract.

Breach of warranty

Breach of a warranty will permit an insurer to repudiate the whole contract. The insurer ceases to have any liability from the date of the breach; if the warranty relates to information provided during contract negotiations then the contract will be void a*b initio* (from the beginning).

If the breach occurs partway through the contract, then the insurer remains liable for any losses prior to the date of the breach.

ABI Statement of General Insurance Practice 1986

This statement, which applies to policyholders insured in a private capacity, has been adopted voluntarily by commercial insurers. It means that an insurer will not refuse to indemnify an insured following a breach of warranty unless the breach and the circumstances of the loss are related or there is evidence of fraud.

Warning

It is good practice to comply with any warranties in insurance policies so that the question of breach does not arise.

Bibliography

Brockelsby, A., *The Way to Profits, Business Interruption Handbook,* Eagle Star Commercial Insurance

Collins, F. W., Freeman, M. A., Jones, F. H., Maclean, K. S., McCallum D. S., *Property & Casualty Claims*, Chartered Insurance Institute (1995), 1 85369 167 4

Dick, J., *Motor Insurance*, Chartered Insurance Institute (1992), 1 85369 131 3

Dickson, G. C. A., Stein W. M., *Insurance Practice,* Chartered Insurance Institute (1991, revised 1996), 1 85369 215 8

Dickson, G. C. A., Stein, W. M., *Risk and Insurance,* Chartered Insurance Institute (1995), 1 85369 182 8

Dickson, G. C. A., Hudson, C. A., *Risk and Insurance with Special Reference to Lloyd's,* Chartered Insurance Institute (1991, revised 1997), 1 85369 211 5

Durrant, J. E., Wilkins. K. R., *Property Insurance Underwriting,* Chartered Insurance Institute (1995), 1 85369 032 5

Edwards, R. W., Few, N., Maxwell, B. Monkman, D. Pow, R. A., *Engineering Insurances and Claims,* Chartered Insurance Institute (1995), 1 85369 197 6

Gamlen, E., Phillips, J., *Business Interruption Insurance Theory and Practice,* Buckley Press Ltd (1992), 0 900236 46 2

General (Non-life), Chartered Insurance Institute (1995), 1 85369 142 9

Insurance, the Market and Legal Principles, Chartered Insurance Institute (1995), 1 85369 137 2

Kluwer Handbook of Insurance, Croner Publications Ltd (1997), 1 870080 13 0, Vols I & II

Körner, W., *The Business Environment,* Chartered Insurance Institute (1995), 1 85369 103 8

Life, Chartered Insurance Institute (1995), 1 85369 147 X

Lloyd's Training Centre, Corporation of Lloyd's, *An Introduction to Lloyd's,* Chartered Insurance Institute, 1 870043 10 3

Maynard, P., *Insurance Broking,* Chartered Insurance Institute (1995), 1 85369 192 5

Parsons, C., Green, D., Mead, M., Körner, W., Steele J., *Company and Contract Law and their Application to Insurance,* Chartered Insurance Institute (1995), 1 85369 187 9

Peck, A. J., *Legal Liabilities*, Chartered Insurance Institute (1995), 1 85369 037 6

Pellatt, A. H., *Private Motor Insurance,* Chartered Insurance Institute (1995), 1 85369 017 1

Pellatt, A. H., Ransom, D. J., *Commercial Motor Insurance,* Chartered Insurance Institute (1995), 1 85369 162 3

Powell, A., *Liability Insurance,* Chartered Insurance Institute (1992), 1 85369 111 9

Ransom, D. J., Bewick, K., James, G. D., Mead, M., Steele J. T., *Legal Aspects of Insurance,* Chartered Insurance Institute (1993), 1 85369 165 8

Smyth, C., *Liability Insurance Practice,* Chartered Insurance Institute (1995), 1 85369 143 7

Way, G. M., Rainbird, J. S., *Property Insurance, Risk Assessment and Control*, Chartered Insurance Institute (1993), 1 85369 027 9

Wildman, P., *Property Insurance,* Chartered Insurance Institute (1996), 1 85369 240 9

Wright, J. D., *Construction Insurance,* Chartered Insurance Institute (1996), 1 85369 210 7